ON

HEGEL

Alison Leigh Brown
Northern Arizona University

WADSWORTH

★

THOMSON LEARNING

Australia • Canada • Mexico • Singapore • Spain
United Kingdom • United States

PROPERTY OF
HIGH POINT PUBLIC LIBRARY
HIGH POINT, NORTH CAROLINA

COPYRIGHT © 2001 Wadsworth, a division of Thomson Learning, Inc.
Thomson Learning™ is a trademark used herein under license.

ALL RIGHTS RESERVED. No part of this work covered by the copyright
hereon may be reproduced or used in any form or by any means—graphic,
electronic, or mechanical, including photocopying, recording, taping, Web
distribution, or information storage and retrieval systems—without the
written permission of the publisher.

Printed in the United States of America
1 2 3 4 5 6 7 04 03 02 01 00

For permission to use material from this text, contact us:
Web: http://www.thomsonrights.com
Fax: 1-800-730-2215
Phone: 1-800-730-2214

For more information, contact:
Wadsworth/Thomson Learning, Inc.
10 Davis Drive
Belmont, CA 94002-3098
USA
http://www.wadsworth.com

ISBN: 0-534-58357-1

PROPERTY OF
HIGH POINT PUBLIC LIBRARY
HIGH POINT, NORTH CAROLINA

Contents

Chapter One: Hegelian System..1
Why Study Hegel?
Hegel's Life and Works
Hegel's Context
The System

Chapter Two: Hegel and the Meaning of Life.........................19
Thinking Philosophically
Coming to Consciousness
Moving to Freedom

Chapter Three: Hegel's Answer to Kant..............................38
Kant
Hegel

**Chapter Four: The Philosopher's Role
In the Analysis of Culture**...57
Hegelian Culture
Hegel's Relationship to Culture
Art
Revealed Religion
Philosophy

Chapter Five: Hegel's Critics..70
Systematic Christianity?
Sexual Difference
Communication of Difference
Revolutionary Inversions
Conclusion

Bibliography..85

1

Hegelian System

Hegelian system purports to have no beginning and no end. It represents a spiraling kind of history which when complete is circular and identical to itself. To start outright with the first step of the system, The Logic, would be wrong for two reasons: first the *Phenomenology of Spirit*, prelude to the system, is the "true" extra-systemic beginning and second one has to explain a multiplicity of prior content and vocabulary to start there. I chose to start with a passage from the *Phenomenology* that captures the historicity of Hegel's thought, its dynamic character, and also its difficulty.

When Hegel is describing the advent of the belief that the world itself has moral qualities, he does so in these words:

> From this determination is developed a moral view of the world which consists in the relation between the absoluteness of morality and the absoluteness of Nature. This relation is based, on the one hand, on the complete *indifference* and independence of Nature towards moral purposes and activity, and, on the other hand, on the consciousness of duty alone as the essential fact, and of Nature as completely devoid of independence and essential being. The moral view of the world contains the development of the moments which are present in this relation of such completely conflicting presuppositions. (*Phenomenology*, 600, pp. 365-366).

This passage implicitly contains many of the interesting propositions people today debate when discussing humanity's joint obligations to the world as opposed to its rational inhabitants. Many of these debates revert to irrationality or even violence because we do not always remember what Hegel tried so hard to express—that every contemporary view contains within it the contradictory, historical perspectives which precede it. This is not, for Hegel, because persons are unable to make up their collective minds but because the truth about the world including nature, consciousness, spirit, substance and propositions is itself is in flux. Truth, for Hegel, is everything: "The True is the whole. But the whole is nothing other than the essence consummating itself through its development" (*Phenomenology*, 20, p. 11). This is not to say that truth is the most important thing, but that the first definition of truth with which we should begin any enquiry is that truth is the totality of existence. In sum, truth is in fact everything.

As a consequence of this definition, for Hegel there are no propositions which retain their meaning or value in a static manner. Thus, in the debate over the possibility of assigning moral rights to say, Redwood trees, Hegel would advise that what is of interest is not finding out the truth about the possibility of trees having rights. Instead, he would urge us to understand all the conflicting legal and moral principles we have held as important with respect to related issues. The synthesis of the best parts of those views is the case for now. An example that he actually gives involves the rights of persons. For Hegel rights in a person are dependent on the totality of the context in which that person finds him or herself. If the person is in a society which predates the notion of rights outside of one sovereign ruler, then that person has no rights in truth. As societies move toward freedom, persons have in fact more right than they did previously. The position does not go both ways, however. Since we live in an age where right (loosely speaking, the law) has included the right, say, to alienate (exchange) private property, persons have that right. A state that does not recognize those rights is henceforth wrong, according to Hegel. So there is no simple relativism; instead, there is a progressive notion of history buoyed up by an analysis of what is known and what has happened in fact.

A difficulty in expositing Hegel is evident. When one reads the preceding paragraph, one could suppose that Hegel could be reduced to a fairly vulgar empiricism or pragmatism. This is, of course, not true. All truth comes together in the end for Hegel and the public, including philosophers, must recognize that in discovering that truth is on the way toward itself and simultaneously in conflict with itself, until that point when it is finished in itself, its job is to see as much of the completed System as it can. In other words, the duty of the philosopher and the citizen in this regard is to see and understand all the contradictions about some state of affairs and synthesize the best, the most true, case. This best case is truth and it will contain contradiction—until the final truth.

This position is historical in the extreme. While there is a posited endpoint, until that endpoint has been reached,

> We must hold to the conviction that it is the nature of truth to prevail when its time has come, and that it appears only when this time has come, and therefore never appears prematurely, nor finds a public that is not ripe to receive it; also we must accept that the individual needs that this should be so in order to verify what is as yet a matter for himself alone, and to experience the conviction, which in the first place belongs only to a particular individual as something universally held. (*Phenomenology*, 71, p. 44).

This method of thinking about truth and its contradictions, we will call dialectical thinking for now. For Hegel, thinking in this way is scientific; indeed, the process of this thinking is science. Its philosophical presentation is system.

Why Study Hegel?

There are many fine introductions to the work of Hegel. What I want to do in this introduction to Hegel is to provide what I believe to be the crucial reasons for continuing to study Hegel. Philosophers, like anything else go in and out of style—there is not a big market right now for say, Malbranche, even though his work was very influential. Hegel's position, thus far outlined, reveals him to be a person who suspends what philosophers call the law of non-contradiction. Basically this law is the law that disallows that both A and not A be the case at the same time. Common sense tells us that the law of non-contradiction is a pretty good description of reality. A pool ball cannot be completely red and completely green. Hegel's suspension of this law causes some philosophers and students of philosophy to throw up their hands and move on to the next Great Thinker. In spite of his apparently illogical starting point, there are three reasons why we should still pay attention to Hegel. The first is that he anchors the world with a sense of purpose which not only makes sense but which is necessary to at least consider in this our only world. What Hegel

3

offers is an understanding of this world as a series of progressive stages toward freedom. Freedom becomes more extensive both in terms of right, or the system of laws, and in terms of individual human consciousness. The discussion of Hegel's contributions to the meaning of life takes place in Chapter Two.

A second reason to maintain an interest in Hegel is because his reading of Kant remains an important epistemological turn in the eschewing of speculation and dualism. There are undoubtedly more easily accessible readings of Kant along similar although independent lines. Hegel's has been influential beyond the halls of academe and thus his reading, however flawed one may find it, has colored the way that many of us view material reality. Many academic fields are dominated by Marxist and post-structuralist categories—sometimes without being conscious of this domination. Both of these ways of thinking are direct, that is explicit reactions against Hegel. This discussion makes up Chapter Three.

Finally, Hegel is self-conscious and articulate about the role of the philosopher with respect to culture, broadly construed. For Hegel, a philosopher has virtually no predictive power. When philosophers engage in future-oriented speculation, they will surely be far from the truth. Hegel argues that philosophers can at best describe what is the case at a particular time and relate it to the history of what is at issue in instructive ways. More important to Hegel than any possible pedagogy, however, is the work that the philosopher does in expressing the truth. This apparently modest role for philosophers is in fact almost preposterously arrogant. The philosopher, having been schooled in system, and recognizing the errors of Kantian epistemology, is the actual speaker of absolute truth. This discussion makes up Chapter Four.

As with any great thinker, Hegel's thoughts can be both dangerous and flawed. Recognizing that the work he was doing outlined a system for cataloguing all possible knowledge, Hegel had a tendency to over generalize his findings. Thus the most common criticism of Hegel is that his system tends toward totalitarian thinking. In Chapter Five we will work through variations of this criticism, sometimes siding with Hegel's critics and sometimes showing the power of Hegel's argument.

It is worth noting that Hegel is extremely difficult. His writing style is universally derided. I have never read a philosopher who finds him to be a master stylist. In addition to a cumbersome method of delivery, his work was conceived as a master system and executed as such. Thus one continuously runs the risk of distorting his position. There are few places where one can feel confident in asserting that this

4

is in fact Hegel's position without indicating a long list of qualifications and directing the reader to the other places within the system where the position is modified by the context of its placement therein. I have opted to forgo this qualifying stance to the extent that I might also remain responsible to the philosopher I not only read first, but who has shaped a considerable part of the ensuing centuries' thinking and political reality.

Hegel's Life and Works

Hegel's Life

Hegel was born August 27, 1770 in Stuttgart. He died in Berlin toward the end of 1831. As Michael Inwood notes there is little in any of Hegel's published work that would give readers an indication of the details of his personal life nor even that the works he is writing are being written by a discrete subjectivity (Inwood, p. 19). Some biographies talk about Hegel as an excellent student, more comment briefly on his undistinguished career as a young student and even through the university. What the reality is about his success as a student is not definitively known. It is of interest that undistinguished students sometimes make disproportionately important intellectual contributions—that strain of thought is best left to biographers.

Hegel left the University in Tubingen in 1793 with his professors noting his prowess in theology and philology but noting also that he had "inadequate knowledge of philosophy" (Lowenberg, x). His two most famous friends were philosopher Schelling, who accused him of criticizing his work in *The Phenomenology of Spirit,* and with whom he subsequently was not friends, and poet Holderlin. His first university post was in Jena where he worked with Schelling; a second was in Heidelberg. In addition to working at universities, he edited a newspaper in Bamberg, tutored wealthy young men, and directed a gymnasium in Nuremburg. When he was not at a university, it was usually for financial reasons. From 1818-1831 he was in Berlin "the acknowledged dictator of one of the most powerful philosophic schools in the history of thought" (Lowenberg, p. xi).

Hegel was devoted to his sister and one place where his private life is revealed, however opaquely, is in his discussions of *Antigone* where his concern for Christiane is evident in his interpretations of that tragedy. He married Marie von Tucher in 1811 and by all accounts their marriage was a happy one. They had two sons who had fulfilling careers of their own. Hegel and his landlady in Jena had a son together, Ludwig Fischer. Marie von Tucher and Hegel adopted Ludwig Fischer when his mother died. There is a novel written about this son (Krell).

While not noted for being a particularly rousing lecturer, Hegel is remembered by his students as a concerned professor. There are few stories about Hegel's social interactions. My favorite involves his encouragement for his students' revolutionary activity. When his students were arrested he took a boat down the river by the jail to wave and show his support; his support would not be extended to substantial matters such as facilitating their release or speaking publicly in their defense.

Hegel's Works

A very good bibliography of works by and about Hegel is found in Beiser, pp. 497-510. Hegel worked within his rigorous system from its inception. One instantiation of that system, reprinted below, gives us a good indication that he believed his most important works to be *The Encyclopedia of Philosophical Sciences, the Science of Logic, The Philosophy of Right, the Lectures on the Philosophy of History, the Lectures on Aesthetics, the Lectures on the Philosophy of Religion,* and the *Lectures on the History of Philosophy,*

It is safe to say that *The Phenomenology of Spirit,* his first major work, is also his most influential. Some commentators view it as a prelude to the mature work which follows. See for example Kainz, pp. 32 ff. Others continue to see it as pivotal. Indeed, there is a huge body of scholarship on Hegel that focuses entirely on only the Preface to the *Phenomenology.* Second to the attention paid to the Preface is that showered on the master/slave dialectic found in the section on self-consciousness in *The Phenomenology of Spirit.* If for no other reason than the attention paid it by Marx, *Philosophy of Right* rivals its younger sibling for influence.

What is interesting about Hegel's work is that he is perhaps the last system builder. Kant's system will be examined in a later section (chapter three). It is enough to say that his is one built on what Hegel thought to be a pure and transcendental vantage point. Kant can never get to the truth of any matter, according to Hegel, because he separates phenomenal from noumenal objects, thereby insuring an insurmountable bridge between knower and known thing and between pure thing (noumenon) and thing as it appears (phenomenon). Hegel's works are all tied up with his conversation to Kant. He saw Kant as advancing thought far beyond his predecessors because he at least attempts to rid his system of speculation; still Hegel believes Kant ultimately fails because he becomes wound up with categories exterior to the world itself.

Spinoza's system is also important to Hegel. As with Kant's system Hegel takes a great deal from Spinoza's. Still, he sees Spinoza's project as ultimately failing because Spinoza holds the meta-rules of mathematics, specifically geometry, as eternal structures. For Hegel, Spinoza's system does not have the ability to accommodate changes in science or history.

Hegel has a method and system that operate similarly to an interactive data base. The truth and falsity of propositions mirror the ones and zeroes of computer functionality in that they say what they mean for this instance of computation but they are extensible and mutable. The categories of analysis cannot, consequently, be held as sacred or untouchable. Novelty must be accounted for and the only manner in which to recognize it is to have the system follow an extensible model.

The works are criticized precisely for generating a system that cannot tolerate novelty. Let us save that criticism for later when we will be in a better position to understand it.

Hegel's Context

Hegel considers it the task of philosophy "to comprehend and not merely to rhapsodize" (Kaufmann, p. 9). Coming on the scene of world history as he does between Kantian reason and a period of heady romanticism, Hegel employs his method of philosophical thinking to forge a synthesis between reason and feeling best expressed as "comprehension".

We like to think that things move quickly in our age of information overload; industries are created to help us deal with the quick pace of our age. It is easy then, for us to overlook that other centuries have been cataclysmic as well. Consider an admittedly idiosyncratic timeline which picks out key moments in history from Kant's birth until Lenin's arrival at Finland Station.

- 1724 Kant is born
- 1770 Hegel is born
- 1781 Kant *Critique of Pure Reason*

7

- 1792-1795 French Revolution in progress, Convention abolished the monarchy, condemns the king to death, supports "a reign of terror"
- 1788 Schopenhauer born
- 1798 Wordsworth *Lyrical Ballads*
- 1801 Richard Trevitick invents and builds the first successful steam vehicle
- 1802 Napoleon becomes consul for life
- 1804 Kant dies; Napoleon crowned emperor
- 1805 Napoleon becomes king of Italy; Issac de Rivaz builds the first vehicle powered by an internal combustion engine; first carbon monoxide air pollution by an automobile.
- 1806 J.S. Mill is born
- 1807 Beethoven *Fifth Symphony*
- 1809 Thomas Paine dies
- 1812 France invades Russia
- 1813 Kierkegaard is born
- 1814-1830 Restoration Monarchy, Louis XVIII grants constitution
- 1816 Divorce abolished in France
- 1818 Karl Marx is born
- 1820 George IV accedes to the throne replacing George III against whom the colonies had rebelled
- 1821 De Quincey *Confessions of an English Opium Eater* published anonymously; Dostoevski is born
- 1823 Beethoven *Ninth Symphony*
- 1827 William Blake dies; Beethoven dies.
- 1830 July Revolution in France
- 1831 Hegel dies
- 1837 Victoria accedes to the throne
- 1840 Zola is born
- 1844 Nietzsche is born
- 1848 First feminist daily in France, "La Voix des Femmes"
- 1855 Kierkegaard dies
- 1860 Schopenhauer dies
- 1864 First International in London
- 1865 Karl Benz designs his first gas-driven vehicle
- 1871 Paris Commune (March through May)
- 1873 J.S. Mill dies
- 1881 Dostoevski dies

- 1883 Marx dies
- 1881 Tsar Aleksandr II assassinated, Tsar Aleksandr III begins his reign; most of Nietzsche's books are banned in Russia
- 1884 Effective French control over Indochina established
- 1889 Nietzsche goes insane
- 1894-1906 Dreyfus Affair
- 1896 Ford and Olds build and test their first models
- 1900 Nietzsche dies
- 1902 Zola dies
- 1917 Lenin arrives at Finland Station

The list shows what a tumultuous time Hegel observed. Revolutions proliferated, many of which have had lasting and profound effects on the landscape of the world and its inhabitants. He finds himself in a political world of shifting boundaries and within a political and artistic milieu which carried the most extreme forms of contradiction. While he had his flirtations with radical political thought in his earlier days, by the time he was filling out the system, he had eschewed the more extreme of his views. The young Hegelians would fight over which Hegel was the good Hegel finding few of the syntheses Hegel urged. Stepelevich marks the end of the heavily politicized Young Hegelian movement occurring in 1846 with the publication of Karl Schmidt's *Das Verstandestum und das Invidiuum* (Stepelevich, p. 15). His analysis is basically that Hegel's "dangerous" views impacted metaphysics, theology, politics, and cultural analysis so dramatically that a flurry of censorship and imprisonment ensued curtailing even the most committed among those affected. Stepelevich cites Nicholas Lobkowicz's statement of the situation:

> Hegel had *idealized* the existing world. His disciples from Strauss to Marx felt forced to translate Hegel's idealizing *description* of the world into a language of *ideals to be achieved.* In the course of this development they also tried to concretize Hegel's abstract idealizations by translating talk about religion into talk about mankind, talk about the sate into talk about existing bourgeois society, etc. Stirner might be described and in any case was understood by Marx as the man who made the final step in this development—a step which leads beyond Hegelian idealism and negates it. For Stirner achieved the final concretization of Hegelianism by reducing

all Hegelian categories to the naked individual self; he denounced not only a certain type of ideal, but all ideals whatsoever (Stepelevich, p. 14).

Hegel's most famous disciple and antagonist, Karl Marx, would reject Hegel but not without taking up his views of dialectic and turning them into a philosophy for concrete change enacted immediately.

The System

In the *Encyclopedia of Philosophical Sciences*, third edition, Hegel outlines the system. The *Science of Logic* is the text meant to explain, or rather flesh out, Logic, the Philosophy of Nature, and the Subjective portion of the Philosophy of Spirit. The *Philosophy of Right* is the text for Objective Spirit through but not including Universal History, whose expansion is outlined in *Lectures on the Philosophy of History*. Absolute Spirit is divided into Art, *Lectures on Aesthetics;* Revealed Religion, *Lectures on the Philosophy of Religion;* and Philosophy, *Lectures on the History of Philosophy*. The reprinted schema is helpful to keep in mind when reading any text by or about Hegel. All of his work in interconnected for him in the way described below. He "saw" the structure while working on *The Phenomenology of Spirit*. After outlining the system and the necessity for it, the rest of his life work was to fill it in.

The position is at first glance preposterous. If taken absolutely seriously, as does, for instance, Kojeve, the conclusions are that for Hegel history is completed. "For if thought is historical, it is only at the end of history that this fact can be known; there can only be knowledge if history at some point stops" (Allan Bloom in Kojeve, p. x). Another way to put this is that "If concrete historical reality is all that the human mind can know, if there is no transcendent intelligible world, then, for there to be philosophy or science, reality must have become rational. The Hegelian solution...is that this has indeed happened and that the enunciation of the universal, rational principles of the rights of man in the French Revolution marked the beginning of the end of history" (Kojeve, p. xi).

There are less extreme interpretations of the consequences of a system that purports to begin from the end. Kojeve's is appealing because it takes Hegel at face value and takes head on the possibility of Hegel having constructed the system, having "seen" it all at once, and realizing the consequences of that vision. Indeed, Kojeve propagates the story that when Hegel saw the totality of knowledge, he sank into a deep depression knowing that he would never again have such a glorious thought and knowing, too, that the rest of his life would be devoted to "filling in the blanks." We can thank Kojeve, however, for asking the question: "What does it mean that one person is able to synthesize the preceding positions and interpretations of history and bring them to bear on current events in such a powerful way?" The question is certainly worth our effort to ask and to ask seriously. If Hegel is right that one can be all knowing, then it follows that people can also be good and free—a not very popular position in either philosophy or common sense discourse. If a finite human being is able to be conscious of knowing an infinite relation, then that finite being is at once finite and infinite. This carries with it a necessary freedom. A more contemporary view that links freedom with infinite possibility is Noam Chomsky's view that human beings have the capacity to construct an infinite variety of sentences. While determined by their material conditions, this capacity is identical with a freedom of generation. For Hegel, this freedom provides capacity for good. That this position is not particularly popular, that man is concretely both good and free, may be dependent on views which describe "men" as naturally evil and free within a larger context of the most free deity.

With the impact of the system—the possibility of positing such a thing—in mind, let us look at what Hegel has proposed.

The System

I. Logic

A. Being
B. Essence
C. Concept

II. Philosophy of Nature

A. Mechanics
B. Physics
B. Organics

III. Philosophy of Spirit

A. Subjective Spirit

B. Objective Spirit
    1. Law
    2. Morality
    3. Sittlichkeit

        a. Family
        b. Civil Society
        c. State
            i.   Constitutional Law
            ii. External Public Law
            iii. Universal History

C. Absolute Spirit

    1. Art
    2. Revealed Religion
    3. Philosophy

To understand Hegel one must examine the system as he outlines it above. As we discuss the various tenets of Hegel's philosophy, I will refer back to this schema. An example of how it works may prove useful. The titles of books and series of lectures occur at the point in Hegel's system where they are both required by system itself and where they are best understood. When we come to study *The Philosophy of Right* we are advised to remember that Hegel viewed it as occurring at the stage of objective spirit. The project of that text is to reconcile the problem of unifying Spirit and Nature. The multiplicity of truths must be brought into a unity of truths. *The Philosophy of Right* begins with Hegel's own contextualization of his work. He writes "*Philosophical manuals are perhaps not now expected to conform to such a pattern, for it is supposed that what philosophy puts together is a work as ephemeral as Penelope's web, one which must be begun afresh every morning*" (p. 1). He is referring to a tradition which depends on what are called "rules and artifices," to which he will not succumb. Instead, he describes what is the case about objective spirit. To do this he must think according to his method:

> After all, the truth about Right, Ethics, and the state is as old as its public recognition and formulation in the law of the land, in the morality of everyday life, and in religion. What more does this truth require—since the thinking mind is not content to possess it in this ready fashion? It requires to be grasped in thought as well; the content which is already rational in principle must win the *form* of rationality and so appear well-founded to untrammeled thinking. Such thinking does not remain stationary at the given, whether the given be upheld by the external positive authority of the state or the *consensus hominum,* or by the authority of inward feeling and emotion and by the 'witness of the spirit' which directly concurs with it. On the contrary, thought which is free starts out from itself and thereupon claims to know itself as united in its innermost being with the truth (*Philosophy of Right,* , p. 3).

This passage contains all the themes discussed so far. The truth is already there moving steadily toward its absolute manifestation. What is required is a formal thinking of that truth that is cognizant but not dependent on state authority, public opinion, sentimental attachment to the Law, or simple faith in God's goodness as ultimate law giver.

Hegel continues in case we misunderstand the limited intent he has for *Philosophy of Right:*

This book, then, containing as it does the science of the state, is to be nothing other than the endeavor to apprehend and portray the state as something inherently rational. As a work of philosophy, it must be poles apart from an attempt to construct a state as it ought to be; it can only show how the state, the ethical universe, is to be understood (*Philosophy of Right*, p. 11).

The interpretative portion of Hegel's work here is to show that the state is in fact *inherently* rational. Hegel is not showing what justice would look like in an ideal world, unlike say Plato, Kant, or in contemporary terms, John Rawls. He is showing that the state *is*. As such it is the best expression of justice.

Hegel does not believe that it is the case for every state in history that it is the best expression of justice. Hegel revered classical Greek society and of the preceding societies, it receives more favor than any other. (He comes by criticisms of Prussian chauvinism honestly—most preceding states are not readily respected by Hegel.) Hegel has reverence for Athenian culture and for Protestant Christianity. Some readers over-emphasize that reverence diluting the fiercely dialectical current of Hegel's work. The constitutional monarchy one finds as a synthesis of increasing freedom, Athenian law, and Christian respect of persons, is the best expression of justice. The earlier manifestations are markedly inferior for him. Charles Taylor expresses Hegel's position here eloquently. He writes:

> It is not likely that Hegel ever thought the task of the age was simply to recover the lost unity of Greek society, or indeed that he ever thought this recovery possible. From the beginning...his thought was polarized as well by the matchless achievement of his own age, the Enlightenment, and by the Christian religion. But this is not to say that he realized all at once at the beginning just what irreversible changes separate us from the ancients and just how profound the opposition was between ancient and modern spirit (Taylor, *Hegel*, p. 65).

If one reads the early essays one can easily imagine Hegel pining for a recovery of ancient Greek civilization. By the time he is writing *Philosophy of Right*, he is more completely devoted to his method.

Hegelian system can be said to be a set of placeholders for content.

Its method is the dialectical method which suspends itself until an endpoint is reached. It has an end-point, posited in time where and when partial truths become actual. Studying Hegel requires remembering that his work fits into a whole in a way that for instance studying a great film maker does not. We can impose a set of themes over the corpus of film maker and this exercise is both instructive and engaging. It makes the study of the films a more exciting endeavor because in addition to viewing discrete works of art one can work into the world of the artist. Other discussants may find this manner of viewing the films confining and even disrespectful to the integrity of the work itself, not to mention the privacy of the artist, to force a body of work into a system. With Hegel, we have no choice but to view his works through his System. Students of Hegel are often told that they have a choice of rejecting Hegel from the outset or to work out criticisms from within. There is not the luxury of finding a flawed argument in some passage and "playing with it." One will get it wrong if one reads Hegel in this manner—piece meal and with reference to say, the theory of the state. The theory of the state is theology, epistemology, moral theory, and parcel of absolute knowing.

At the end of *The Phenomenology of Spirit* Hegel describes the revelation of *the absolute Notion,* or the coming to knowledge of Spirit that contrary to appearances of fresh starts, each stage of history and of consciousness carries the history of its development inside it. He writes:

> This revelation is, therefore, the raising-up of its depth, or its *extension,* the negativity of this withdrawn 'I', a negativity which is its externalization or its substance; and this revelation is also the Notion's Time, in that this externalization is in its own self externalized, and just as it is in its extension, so it is equally in its depth, in the Self. The *goal,* Absolute Knowing, or Spirit that knows itself as Spirit, has for its path the recollection of the Spirits as they are in themselves and as they accomplish the organization of their realm. Their preservations, regarded from the side of their free existence appearing in the form of contingency, is History; but regarded from the side of their [philosophically] comprehended organization, it is the Science in the sphere of appearance : the two together, comprehended History, form alike the inwardizing and the Calvary of absolute Spirit, the actuality, truth, and certainty of his throne, without which he would be lifeless and alone. Only

15

from the chalice of this realm of spirits
foams forth for Him his own infinitude
(Schiller's *Die Freundschaft, ad fin.*)
(*Phenomenology of Spirit,* 808, p. 493).

This passage contains the barebones of system. System, science, has as its task the stepping outside of itself to understand the progression of personal and cultural development. Kojeve reads the project Hegel sets for us in understandable terms:

As for the goal of History—it is *Wissen,* Knowledge of self—that is, Philosophy (which finally becomes Wisdom). Man creates an historical World only in order to know what this World is and thus to *understand* himself in it(Kojeve, p. 162).

A good disciple, he does not separate out individual consciousness in his description. Instead Philosophy itself becomes Wisdom, and "Man," a collective designator is the understanding thing. As is often the case with Hegel one wants to ask commonsensical questions such as "Is it not the case that only individuals 'know' anything? How can an abstraction, such as Philosophy, understand itself as anything?" These questions help us to see what Hegel is doing with system. Philosophy is not an abstraction for Hegel. It is the sum total of all thinking beings who have engaged in that practice: it is a living thing. Kojeve is helpful again:

Hegel does not need a God who would reveal the truth to him. And to find the truth, he does not need to hold dialogues with 'the men in the city,' or even to have a 'discussion' with himself or to 'meditate' *a la Descartes.* (Besides no purely verbal discussions, no solitary meditation can lead to the truth, of which Fighting and Work are the only 'criteria.') He can find it all alone, while sitting tranquilly in the shade of those 'trees' which taught Socrates nothing, but which teach Hegel many things about themselves and about men. But all this is possible only because there *have been* cities in which men had discussions against a background of fighting and work, while they worked and fought for and because of their opinions (Kojeve, p. 186).

Kojeve is an important commentator on Hegel. (His students include psychoanalyst Jacques Lacan, librarian-novelist-philosopher George Bataille, phenomenologist Merleau-Ponty, and others.) Still his interpretations are controversial. He is relentless in his making Hegelian system one which only concerns humanity because he reads the "pantheism" of the Hegelian system as reducible to what most traditional thinkers about religion would call "atheism." On this point, namely that Hegel's system is important precisely because he brings concrete reality into the world of the idea, he is consistent with more conventional scholars of Hegel.

Charles Taylor is an exceptionally insightful reader of Hegel. His explanation of how we can collectively come to knowledge is especially illuminating and in good systemic manner links the exposition of Hegel to a particular time, historical period, and philosophical context:

> Thus these four transpositions in Hegel's position which take place around the time he goes to Jena and carry through the Jena period into his mature position are related: the acceptance of separations as part of the ultimate unity, the shift to philosophy as the crucial medium, the shift from a man-centered theory to one centered on *Geist*, and the notion that man's realization is not planned by him, but can only be recognized post hoc. The first two are linked through Hegel's sense of the connection between separation and autonomy, autonomy and rationality; the opposition between autonomy and expressive unity leads him to a notion of *Geist* as greater than man, and *Geist* as the subject of history transforms his view of history. Man's task is now to recognize, and to recognize clearly, not by a cloudy intuition which would deny his vocation to rational autonomy; and thus the apex of human realization, which turns out to be the realization of *Geist*, lies in philosophical awareness (Taylor, *Hegel*, p. 74).

Our work is cut out for us. In clear headed fashion we must give up a certain kind of self-importance we have associated with autonomy and rationality and proceed from a position of shared rationality and autonomy. In doing this, we will have a greater share, ultimately of both.

This is a good place for us to make the transition to Hegel's existential moment. It would be natural to suppose that the meaning of an individual's life is lessened within a system that appears to favor objectivity over subjectivity. As we examine Hegel's answers to the perennial question: "What is the meaning of life?" we might see that Subjectivity does not erase subjectivity.

2
Hegel and the Meaning of Life

We have laid the groundwork for analyzing the first of the reasons for maintaining an interest in Hegel today.   Hegel offers good argumentation that there is meaning in human existence but he is not content to spell out a few prescriptions for how an individual, or indeed a collection of citizens, should act.   The closest he comes to such didacticism is found in the often cited "Reason is purposive action." That phrase carries an implicit presupposition that one should act purposively because one is capable of possessing freedom.   To be accountable for one's life and actions within a framework of changing perspectives, which framework has an immutable telos, requires a way of thinking that cannot begin outside of real (dynamic) truth.   That is, it cannot begin with antecedent propositions unchanged by the tempest of time.   In a sense, Hegel asks us to begin in the middle of things:

> From its very beginning, culture must leave room for the earnestness of life in its concrete richness; this leads the way to an experience of the real issue.   And even when the real issue has been penetrated to its depths by serious speculative effort, this kind of knowing and judging will still retain its appropriate place in ordinary conversation.
>
> The true shape in which truth exists can only be the scientific system of such truth.   To help bring philosophy closer to the form of Science, to the goal where it can lay aside

the title '*love* of knowing' and be *actual* knowing—that is what I have set myself to do (*Phenomenology of Spirit*, 4-5, p. 3).

Hegel's task is no less than to make philosophy science, and not mere science but the science of true understanding. To follow him on the way to such understanding, we must examine dialectical thought in more detail.

Thinking Philosophically

We began this essay by opining about the various views persons might hold about "natural rights" and to what sorts of things we might legitimately assign them. The philosophical debates about such things as rights and justice are not often taught or studied as part and parcel of the very bloody events which work the ideas out in history. The advent of "area studies" such as women's studies and ethnic and race studies has done much to make clear that there is a direct correlation between John Locke's pristine writings about the inability of so-called savages to mix their labor with land and subsequent genocide. Hegel is a forerunner of making theory accountable, indeed, identical with the history it makes and tells. And like the best of area studies a Hegelian position allows one to respect Locke for the power of the arguments against the divine rights of kings while abhorring his continued belief that not all people are those who are created equally. Tellingly, it forces the reader of texts to address the entire text. Once during a philosophical conversation about Hegel, an interlocutor ventured, "Yes, but sexism aside," at which point the better student of Hegel refused to consider Hegel with the sexism suspended. It is integral to the description of the time and if ignored becomes more insidious—as indeed it has done.

What may seem an unlikely aside into "politics" and university curricula is in fact crucial to getting a grip on Hegel. If the thinking self is allowed (or rather gives itself permission) to pick and choose what is thought, there is less free thought taking place, and hence less meaning. Hegel never lost sight of the identity relation between theory and action and hence the radical accountability a person has for the way in which he or she does theory and the way in which he or she sees the world. If a person proclaims that "my life has no meaning," Hegel believes that it is that person's fault and that the person is dissembling, that is, being dishonest. Meaning is there and failing to acknowledge this is shirking responsibility to the point of lying.

Thinking philosophically, then is as much a ethical act as an epistemological one. It takes account of the interconnectedness of the various branches of philosophical, theological, and scientific thought. Charles Taylor writes on this issue:

> It is in Germany, where actual revolution takes place simply as an import, along with the invading French armies, that the millenarist expectations are philosophically elaborated. In the process they are transposed, reflecting not so much the hopes of the radical Enlightenment as those of the expressivist theory of nature as source. What emerges is the spiral view of history...in which we break out of our original integration into the great current of life, to enter a phase of division and opposition, followed by a return to unity at a higher level.
>
> Hegel incorporates the whole traditional scenario of Western millenarism, but in a transposed, philosophical form. There are the three ages of world history, the crisis of heightened conflict at the entry of the new age (fortunately now behind us, in the form of the Revolution and its resulting wars), and the new higher resolution. Lost in the philosophical transposition, of course, is the final battle between good and evil, resulting in the total victory of the former. The Hegelian battle is never between good and bad, but between two requirements of the good; and it issues in synthesis, not total victory" (Taylor, *Sources of the Self,* p. 388).

How can one be accountable for the meaning of one's life? Hegel doesn't offer blueprints, not being that sort of philosopher. Indeed, he may even scoff at the question, asking one to consider instead how one might understand Science. But even that is overly prescriptive. What Hegel does is to describe two meaningful accounts of human existence: that of an individual coming to consciousness of itself as self-consciousness and that of World Spirit coming to know itself as the totality of relations. In contemporary culture the first account spawns existentialism and phenomenology while the latter is the beginning of class analysis. Let's turn to the individual's journey first, noting in one of the qualifications I promised to make as rarely as possible, that there are Hegel scholars who assert that discussions of individual journeys are an after the fact construction by readers of Hegel who are insufficiently scientific.

Coming to Consciousness

People who study Hegel are prone to make the same sorts of outrageous pronouncements that Hegel does—a trait that is either endearing or annoying to those who hear or read them. Two such pronouncements belong to Kojeve who asserts "There is only one dilemma: Plato or Hegel," and Hyppolite who no less grandly asserts "What is at issue here is all human experience." Let's look at each of them in turn.

Kojeve

When Kojeve poses the central dilemma as that between Plato or Hegel he means essentially that between theology or philosophy. He writes:

> Now, we are faced with a fact. A man who is clearly not mad, named Hegel, claims to have realized Wisdom. Therefore, before deciding for or against Philosophy or Theology—that is, for or against the assertion of the impossibility of realizing Wisdom—we must see whether or not Hegel was right in asserting that he is a Wise Man, whether through his very being he has not already settled once and for all the question that interests us.
>
> And in order to resolve this question we must see: (1) if the current state of things actually corresponds to what for Hegel is the perfect State and the end of History; and (2) if Hegel's Knowledge is truly circular (Kojeve, pp. 96-97).

Kojeve decides on, and then argues strenuously for, the proposition that the question is settled. Hegel is a Wise Man. He is able to affirm Hegel's wisdom by showing that Hegel finishes the making absolute of humanity; that is, for Kojeve what Hegel has done is to show that the end of history is in fact the end of a humanity that must continuously transform itself into an other, specifically an infinite being whose infinity is drawn from radical alterity, God. Up until Hegel described what was already the case about humanity, that by annihilating their power and possibilities to an unknowable and unattainable other, humanity could not be conscious of itself as in time. After Hegel saw system in the scientific way that we have discussed what remained for humanity was a view of itself as a time-bound, finite humanity. It is when humanity so recognizes itself that it can simultaneously recognize

22

that knowledge is truly circular.

Kojeve's argument for his position is complicated. A truncated version goes like this. First Kojeve must tie the end of history thesis with the perfect state thesis. The perfect state is the state that is utterly in truth, that is, the state that instantiates every possible configuration of justice. The end of history thesis is that which, inextricably bound up with the perfect state thesis, avers that since the perfect state has been realized, nothing new will happen. As we saw Hegel, after "realizing" that he had thought System scientifically, also realized that he would never have another thought of such import. Similarly when the revolution succeeded over Napoleon, no conflict could be a new conflict. Here is Kojeve's analysis.

> For we certainly cannot assert, on the basis of attempts already made, that the State in question is impossible *in principle.* Now if this State is possible, Wisdom is also possible. And then no need to abandon Philosophy and take flight into some Religion or other; hence no need to subordinate the consciousness that I have of myself to a coming to consciousness of what I am not: of God, or of some inhuman perfection (esthetic or other), or of race, people, or nation (Kojeve, p. 97).

It is possible then that the existing state is the finished, or perfect, state. As such humanity is only itself, it has no larger possibility outside of itself. Kojeve argues that when Hegel sees this he sees that he must give up individuality. That is absolute Knowledge demands a necessary abandonment of individuality per se. The individuality which must be rejected is the individuality which carries its enlightenment autonomy in itself as a gift from something other than itself. The new individuality is conscious of itself as having its particularity from the universal: "And becoming a Wise Man by that final acceptance of death, he [Hegel] published a few years later the First Part of the "System of Science," entitled "Science of the Phenomenology of the Spirit," in which he definitively reconciles himself with all that is and has been, by declaring that there will never more be anything new on earth" (Kojeve, p. 168).

It is uncharitable to read Hegel as erasing interiority. That may be a consequence of a chain of reason but if the chain of reason is followed what has happened is an exchange of one kind of consciousness for another. It is not that Hegel sees System as devouring discrete subjectivity. Instead, by disallowing the meaning of life's genesis in something outside of System, interiority is conscious of itself as a thing which dies. Its interiority, henceforth, is contingent on its development and the working out of its own desires. Those desires change as systems changes. What had been viewed as consciousness was in fact an illusion. Kojeve explains this in these words:

> Man's definitive satisfaction, which completes History, necessarily implies *consciousness* of individuality that has been realized (by universal recognition of particularity). And this consciousness necessarily implies consciousness of death. If, then, Man's complete satisfaction is the goal and the natural end of history, it can be said that history completes itself by Man's perfect understanding of his death. Now, it is in and by Hegelian Science that Man for the first time has fully understood the phenomenological, metaphysical, and ontological meaning of his essential finiteness. Therefore, if this Science, which is Wisdom, could appear only at the end of History, only through it is History perfected and definitively completed. For it is only by understanding himself in this Science as mortal—that is, as a historical free individual—that Man attains fullness of consciousness of a self that no longer has any reason to negate itself and become other (Kojeve, p. 258).

The implications of these conclusions to an individual's understanding of the meaning of life are varied. One could withdraw into morbid passivity. It is this consequence which alarms famous critics of Hegel such as Kierkegaard and Nietzsche. One could alternatively suppose that one's political import was so negligible that one should acquiesce in whatever political formation exists. This consequence is the one Marx is concerned to counter by making system material rather than ideal. Another implication is that one is more fully empowered as an individual because one sees things in truth. This is the implication Kojeve believed was the most rational conclusion. Whichever implications the reader finds to follow, he or she will see that the working out of these implications make up a significant portion of the ethical content of existentialist, Marxist, post-structuralist, and phenomenological thought. A major thread through these theories is that humanity is responsible for itself. This seems to be a good place for humanity to begin its philosophizing about the meaning of life.

Hyppolite

Being (existence) and time are central concepts to philosophies dealing with the meaning of life. From Heidegger to Beauvoir, twentieth century philosophers have struggled with what can be the case about individuals within the confines of our existence and our temporal nature. A very different scholar of Hegel than Kojeve is his contemporary, Hyppolite. Hyppolite discusses the concepts we are struggling with by detailing religious consciousness, the predecessor to philosophical consciousness, as follows:

> What is at issue here is all human experience: theoretical, practical, esthetic, and religious. Human experience allows the self to discover itself and substance to reveal itself to the self. This experience necessarily takes place in time for within consciousness 'the whole, although not conceived of, precedes its moments' (PE, II, 305; PG, 558; PM, 800). Thus the concept appears to consciousness as an *unfulfilled requirement*, as the self which is still outside itself and in a sort of ex-tasy in relation to self. The point is that the substance which presents itself as the object of consciousness is not yet conceived of, that is, does not pertain to the self; it must be developed in an experience which links it to self-consciousness, to the concept, but then this concept is present as a possible experience. That is why 'time is the very concept that is there and that presents itself to consciousness as a vacant intuition.' Time is thus the disquiet of consciousness which has not attained itself, which sees its self a outside itself" (Hyppolite, p. 579).

Hyppolite weaves individual consciousness with absolute spirit throughout his exegesis. Furthermore, being a very cautious and careful scholar, he reads Hegel as Hegel asks to be read: within the context of the system. Thus, Hegel sees religious consciousness as something taken up explicitly by absolute spirit and he offers the system which tells us to examine each work where it appears in the progression of actual Absolute Spirit working itself out. Thus Hyppolite is diligent in forcing our reading into not only the structure of the *Phenomenology of Spirit,* but also through the system itself. He reminds us that "Absolute knowledge can only appear when the actual history of the world spirit has led it to consciousness of itself" (Hyppolite, p. 601). For that eventuality spirit must pass through the stages of Logos, Nature, and Spirit. Critics of system scoff at Hegel's

25

positioning of Nature has coming out of logic. Hyppolite defends Hegel like this:

> Logos and nature mutually presuppose each other; one cannot be posed without the other. It is absurd to imagine a causality of any kind in logos which would produce nature...In the same way, one cannot say that Hegel deduces nature from logos, unless we change the usual meaning of the word 'deduction.'...Logos is the whole which negates itself as nature, it is the abstraction of pure thought which poses itself as pure thought and in this posing of itself excludes nature. Now, we have already said that this abstraction—which is negativity itself—was not the work of a simple human understanding, but that it was at the very heart of the absolute. The absolute exists only in this negativity" (Hyppolite, p. 602).

Hyppolite does not see absolute spirit as the sum total of human consciousness as Kojeve does. Instead, he places absolute spirit in negativity, or that which produces the movement of the system. For things to progress, there must be tension or conflict. The absolute exists in negativity. Spirit is able to come on the scene, as Spirit, when logic and nature enter into history.

> The sequence of these spirits which succeed each other in time is *history*. Seen from the viewpoint of their conceptual organization it is the science of phenomenal knowledge (*phenomenology*). The unity of these two aspects, which Hegel distinguishes from "phenomenology" properly speaking, yields a philosophy of history, conceived history, and this history, far from being a digression, something separate from absolute spirit, an itinerary in God which would not concern God himself, "on the contrary constitutes actuality, the truth and the certainty of [absolute spirit's]
>
> throne, without which [spirit] would be a lifeless solitude" (Hyppolite, p. 605-606).

For Kojeve the meaning of life is enriched by an understanding that one is able to partake of absolute spirit in truth. One's consciousness, thus, remains open to extra-systemic communion but in a heightened manner. One knows that one is a part of an ever changing march through history not as a puppet of God, but as an active participant. Each of the commentators we have discussed see Hegel as pivotal in coming to terms with the contradictions thinkers had encountered because of the richness of cultural heritage which was culminating in aesthetic, cultural and political upheavals. Fearing that humanity was hurting itself by insufficient attention to history, history's lesson, and the wisdom of its predecessors, these thinkers pinpoint the significance of Hegel's cold portrayal of spiraling history. One could argue easily and forcefully that our contemporary culture requires attention to meaning in this comprehensive sense now more than then.

Moving to Freedom

Meaning can be found, then, by teasing out the puzzles concerning individuals' relationship to concepts larger than themselves. These affairs for Hegel cannot be private matters but must be thought of in terms not only of our contemporary communities but also in conjunction with the history of thought and state. There are those who would argue that the history of the last century, which Hegel did not know, condemns us to thinking in solely political terms. The devastations we have occasioned on each other don't leave time for private musings about our personal responsibilities. Instead, we should concern ourselves with political (or social) action now. Hegel is important here largely for his theory of history and philosophy of law which, if not in intent, in practice stands as the foundation of political theories which urge the recognition that changes in consciousness are the sine qua non of any political movement. Class consciousness as the mover of class conflict can be traced directly to Hegel's interplay between objective and subjective spirit with respect to history. Let us examine the major text of this discussion in this context.

The *Philosophy of Right*, as we have noted, is Hegel's attempt to reconcile the problem of unifying Spirit and Nature. That is, Absolute Spirit, the totality of all relations of contradiction and identity, comes complete with contradictions. The Absolute, then, is non-transcendent, it is not a thing in itself but an entity moving towards its own self unity. The philosophy of "Right" must then, occur in objective spirit because it is the body of rules and actualities coming from the multiplicity of opinions and actions at the level of subjective spirit. When the objective and subjective spirits can overcome their apparent contradictions in a unity that is expressive of freedom, they will have merged toward absolute spirit.

27

Philosophy should be concerned neither with prescriptions nor with individual constructions. For Hegel, "To comprehend what is, this is the task of philosophy, because what is, is reason. Whatever happens, every individual is the child of his time; so philosophy too is its own time apprehended in thoughts" (*Philosophy of Right,* p. 11). Philosophy cannot prescribe because philosophy comes only "when actuality is already there cut and dried after its process of formation has been completed" (pp. 12-13). Hegel sets out to describe "Right" as it is not as it should be. The circular nature of his thought makes it very difficult to exposit just one theme. Throughout that is what I have done and what I will do. The reader of even an introductory text to Hegel should see a work from start to finish. Because of its notoriety through Marx but more importantly because legal and civil society are more familiar to most of us than the intricacies of epistemology, I have chosen this text to cover in its entirety. This is not to say that it is covered thoroughly; still, it will give a good idea of how Hegel lays out a text.

All his texts are divided in triads. This is because the dialectical method of thinking follows the dominant tyrant of negativity. For every thing, including philosophical positions, that arises, there will arise something else which contradicts or negates it. As the two things work themselves out a synthesis of their best parts will arise. We just noted the progression from logic to nature to spirit. In the text at hand we will go from abstract right to morality to ethical life. Until the last two decades, English speakers taught this progression as thesis, anti-thesis, synthesis. You will encounter many helpful analyses of Hegel using this terminology. It is misleading, however, for two reasons. First the word "thesis" makes us think mostly of well-argued for positions. Hegel meant the first stage to cover every sort of thought thing. Second, anti-thesis implies a clean logical category, which negation is not.

A little more background about Hegelian terminology and method is needed before we turn to the text. Four definitions are essential to our reading.

1. A thing thought, for Hegel, is what the Understanding sees as universal when it is mere abstraction.

2. A concept is what Reason thinks concretely.

3. An Idea is a concept synthesized with the thing thought. What is actual is essence plus existence; it is abstraction together

28

with concreteness. For Hegel, "the subject matter of the philosophical science of right is the Idea of right, that is, the concept of right together with the actualization of that concept" (p. 14). The task of this philosophy is to look on the immanent development of the thing itself.

4. Right, itself, is positive in general when it has the form of being valid in a State; Right acquires positivity in its content if the rational character relates necessarily to natural history, it is universalizable, and it has a body of law (pp. 15-16).

What Hegel wants to delineate for his readers is the Idea of Right.

There is no right without will. "The basis of mind is, in general, mind; its precise place and point of origin is the will" (p. 20). The will for Hegel contains two contradictory moments. On the one hand the will contains an element of pure indeterminacy—in this guise, the will is abstract negativity. On the other hand the will is ego which by definition places it in transition. The will here is concrete negativity. The definition of will is the will which is the unity of abstract and concrete negativity. Hegel explains the relation of these moments of the will like this:

> Every self-consciousness knows itself (i) as universal, as the potentiality of abstracting from everything determinate, and (ii) as particular, with a determinate object, content, and aim. Still, both these moments are only abstractions; what is concrete and true (and everything true is concrete) is the universality which has the particular as its opposite, but he particular which by its reflection into itself has been equalized with the universal (p. 23).

What the will looks toward in the first place will be immediate. In this phase it is free only in itself or for an external observer. The will must have itself as its object before it can be for itself what is already in itself. This pull in two directions results in impulsive pronouncements about the state of people in their willing. One can posit from some of the data that people are naturally good and from other data that they are naturally evil. This leads to confusion over what we are and of what we are capable. The truth of the matter for Hegel is that in the process of comprehending the contradiction in will, we come to be increasingly free. At the point where the contradiction is unified in freedom, we are free. So for instance, when Hegel recognizes this point, he shows that there is no possibility of just (lawful) institutions henceforth which begin with a lack of recognition of this sacred freedom. The enslavement of human beings by other human beings is absolutely wrong in his view after that point where it is recognized that Freedom is an Idea. "An existent of any sort embodying the free will, this is what right is. Right therefore is by definition freedom as Idea" (p. 33).

The division of the subject matter of the philosophy of right follows the analysis of will. The will is immediate as personality. The embodiment of that abstract personality is abstract or formal right, which makes up the first portion of Hegel's text. The will reflected from its external embodiment into itself is embodied in morality, the second portion. Will in its absolutely universal existence is the basis of ethical life. Here Hegel shows such willing in its three stages: as natural mind, or the family, in its divisions as civil society, and as State, or Freedom, which is further divided into the mind of a nation, international politics, and world history.

Abstract Right

Abstract Right is divided up in a way familiar to all first year law students or students of the philosophy of law. The categories included are property, contracts, and torts, or what Hegel calls wrongs. In this category of "wrong" Hegel includes crimes. Let's go through these remembering that our aim in going through this text is not just to experience Hegel's philosophy of right but more to asses what of importance remains in this classifying for us specifically as it relates to our coming to freedom as individuals and as members of States or collectives.

For Hegel, right is always with respect to a person. Personality means a person who is completely determined and who has knowledge of oneself as infinite and free. To translate this we can rethink it in terms of Hegel's vocabulary of the subjective and objective sides of things. At the level of abstract right a person is determined due to its thingly and sometimes capricious nature but it is conscious of itself as capable of being, and hence actually, free.

> Personality implies that as *this* person: (i) I am completely determined on every side (in my inner caprice, impulse, and desire, as well as by immediate external facts) and so finite, yet (ii) none the less I am simply and solely self-relation, and therefore in finitude I know myself as something infinite, universal, and free. An imperative accrues to each person under abstract right "Be a person and respect others as persons

30

(p. 37).

Property arises within these contexts and can only be property of right if it is a mere thing. There is, for Hegel, an absolute appropriation of people over things. He is what might be called today a speciest: people are the most important category and the only types of things that can have any dominion over other kinds of things. A person can put its will into anything, this is its role and consequently cannot be hindered by things in its appropriation.

Possession means having the power over a thing *ab extra*. For Hegel there is no qualification on this definition. Possession cannot be related to need but only to putting one's will in something else. Possessions become private property like this: "Since my will, as the will of a person, and so as a single will, becomes objective to me in property, property acquires the character of private property" (p. 42). For Hegel what is possessed and how much is possessed must be indifferent to right. The modifications of property cannot be sullied with any consideration but the relation of will to thing.

There are three relations of will to thing as property. First one takes possession and this is a positive action. Second, one uses the thing. This is a negative action. Finally one may alienate the thing—this relation is infinite. With respect to the first relation, as the State evolves, for Hegel, slavery becomes impossible. The positive action of taking possession imposes the form of the will on the object. The full argument is lengthy. The point for Hegel is that justifications for slavery necessarily fail because they regard man as a natural entity—a characterization Reason must reject. Arguments for the absolute injustice of slavery are equally invalid for Hegel because they depend on a concept that man is inherently free. Hegel notes that freedom has not been a constant staple in the course of history. Instead, he argues that having been thought under the concept of State, slavery is impossible. There is no discussion for him. So long as wills exercised themselves as merely taking possession, we mark something as ours only and there is no progression toward freedom.

When we use property we are making a negative judgment of the will on the thing: "The use of the thing is my need being externally realized through the change, destruction, and consumption of the thing. The thing thereby stands revealed as naturally self-less and so fulfills its destiny" (p. 49). Alienation is the selling of the thing or its exchange and contains an infinite judgment on it: "The reason I can alienate my property is that it is mine only in so far as I put my will

31

into it" (p. 52). Criticisms of these divisions occur in Chapter five.

There are going to be more than one will and as such the wills will conflict—particularly over property. Contracts arise as a means of mediating the exchange of property. Two areas where Hegel maintains that contracts are not appropriate are in marriage and with respect to citizens and their relation to the state. The marriage relation as a contract is as impossible as slavery. Marriage, for Hegel, is about self-recognition and the relation folds only onto itself. Furthermore, the contract is always a private matter and for the citizen to be expected to contract with the State is to blur private and civic spaces.

Wills on occasion will be at variance with the universal. These willings are what Hegel calls "wrong" (p. 64). There are two important points in Hegel's discussion of wrong. First he puts Crime and Tort together—the point of contact being that wrong "transgresses abstract right and is an exercise of force against the existence of my freedom in an external thing" (p. 67). Secondly in rectifying wrong, the State only has the abstract right to restore itself. Punitive use of force, is for Hegel, wrong whether against non-malicious wrong or wanton crime. "The sole positive existence which the injury possesses is that it is the particular will of the criminal. Hence to injure (or penalize) this particular will as a will determinately existent is to annul the crime, which otherwise would have been held valid and to restore the right" (p. 69).

Moving from Right to Morality involves a negation of the negation. "The will first puts itself in the opposition between the implicit universal will and the single explicitly independent will, and then, through the supersession of this opposition (through the negation of the negation) it determines itself as a will so that it is a free will not only in itself but for itself also" (p. 74). As the will becomes for itself, it can see itself as involved in more and more self-relations where abstract law is not required to keep desire in check. The personality of the will is now its object: "the infinite subjectivity of freedom, a subjectivity become explicit in this way, is the principle of the *moral* standpoint" (p. 74).

Morality

As a second term, this section is very short. Hegel deals extensively with Morality in the *Phenomenology of Spirit*, if one is interested in constructing a full moral theory according to Hegel. Here he discusses three areas: Purpose and Responsibility, Intention and Welfare, and Good and Conscience. In the sphere of morality we act. "The externalization of the subjective or moral will is action" (p. 78).

32

Purpose, where responsibility is abstract and this short section is one of classification. Morality for many of us is connected to duty. Duty resides in individuals' inner content and the right here is of expected welfare within limits of rationality. Consequently, rights exist only for free entities. The rights one free entity exerts over another are absolute and clear for Hegel. If another is in distress, for example, one is duty bound to alleviate that distress as an abstract duty to the right in the other—it is not a question of mercy. The content of morality is for Hegel subjective universality, or the good. The good is sometimes wickedness sometimes conscience. "The good is thus freedom realized, the absolute end and aim of the world" (p. 86). Each particular will sees the essence of its will as good. As such duty must be universal else duties would be willy nilly assigned to preference.

> Because every action explicitly calls for a particular content and a specific end, while duty as an abstraction entails nothing of the kind, the question arises: what is my duty? As an answer nothing is so far available except: (a) to do the right, and (b) to strive after welfare, one's own welfare, and welfare in universal terms, the welfare of others (p. 89).

Subjective universality contains subjectivity and as such will not be absolutely reasonable. Thus, on occasion instead of conscience exerting itself toward the good, wickedness will exert itself toward wrong. This is part and parcel of the good and is crucial to our freedom.

Morality concerns itself with the well-being of individuals. Ethical Life concerns itself with the well-being of states. Moral considerations are secondary in Ethical Life.

Ethical Life

Ethical Life is divided into three areas: family, civil society, and the state. Family includes marriage, family capital, and the education of children at which point there is dissolution of the family. Civil Society includes the system of needs, the administration of justice, and the police and corporation. The State is divided into constitutional law, international law, and world history.

These areas of right are justifiable because as institutions they are the groundwork for actual freedom for concrete, particular individuals. Hegel writes

> The right of individuals to be subjectively destined to freedom

is fulfilled when they belong to an actual ethical order, because their conviction of their freedom finds its truth in such an objective order, and it is in an ethical order that they are actually in possession of their own essence or their own inner universality (p. 109).

Here and only here are rights attached to specific duties. In the sphere of abstract right an individual has a right but another has the corresponding duty. In morality, the coming together of right and duty is desired but there is no force requiring it. Within the sphere of ethical life, the rights and duties come together in one person with force.

The family is ethical mind in its natural phase. As we noted, marriage is not a contract. It begins in a contract in ethical life, but only so that its contractual nature can be superceded. The duty to children is threefold and for Hegel may be enforced by the State. Basically parents are obliged to feed, educate and love their children. The members of a family dissolve into civil society when they become particulars of civil society—as opposed to being members in a family. Remaining steeped in the notions of ethical life propounded by Aristotle, Hegel sees man as that which "has substantive life in the state, in learning, and so forth, as well as in labour and struggle with the external world and with himself" (p. 114) while woman "has her substantive destiny in the family, and to be imbued with family piety is her ethical frame of mind" (p. 114). The break away to civil society then is a male prerogative (and duty) while women apparently remain members of families with no entry to civil society.

One begins to see in Ethical Life why so many wish to reject Hegel outright, instead of criticizing him from the inside. Civil Society is the space where concrete needs of particular individuals are sometimes engaged in struggle and other times working merrily in harmony. Women readers, and their friends, may be less enthusiastic about all this struggle and laborious good will than earlier in the text and all of us may begin to ask ourselves who else is missing from all this industry and bustling activity.

Economic life, or the system of needs is the first stage of Civil Society. Hegel delineates the various classes and the duties assigned to each of them. Because the system of needs will inevitably end in well-intentioned stalemate, the administration of justice is a required element of Civil Society. One of the areas which most demands justice is the overcoming of prejudice.

It is part of education, of thinking as the consciousness of the single in the form of universality, that the ego comes to be apprehended as a universal person in which all are identical. A man counts as a man in virtue of his manhood alone, not because he is a Jew, Catholic, Protestant, German, Italian, &c. This is an assertion which thinking ratifies and to be conscious of it is of infinite importance. It is defective only when it is crystallized, e.g. as a cosmopolitanism in opposition to the concrete life of the state (p. 134).

I quote that entire passage for two reasons. Throughout I have kept Hegel's male pronouns and language. At this point in the text, it is clear that I have done this because he does not mean he or she. When it is ambiguous I have used "it" or "one" as he often does. This is a point about understanding Hegel. Second it is important I think to see Hegel "seeing" that equality must be comprehensive. It follows from his arguments against, e.g. slavery. Still, I have seen that passage quoted without the last sentence. I leave it to the reader to interpret it.

The theory of law in this section is very interesting and contains many lessons our legal system could learn from. Hegel argues forcefully that no act of revenge is justified in or outside of a legal system. He believes us to have duty with respect to the law so if law allows itself to be "wrong" we must see that as "only right implicit" (p. 141). Furthermore laws must be administered identically in every case. (He details a very limited executive privilege in the section on State.

To enforce law and to protect private property, police and corporations are necessary. The police is most needed when poverty arises because of paucity of work. The corporation, akin to a guild or union for Hegel, arises so that families can be guaranteed a stable basis on which to build their home. The Corporation is to ethical life as the family is to morality.

Finally we arrive at the state. Basically for Hegel The state forces the sacrifice of the individual pursuit of needs and the subsumption into the ideal is satisfying for the individual. Since the system of needs arises from actual concrete needs of men, the state is an instantiation of the rational. "The state is absolutely rational inasmuch as it is the actuality of the substantial will which it possesses in the particular self-consciousness once that consciousness has been raised to consciousness of its universality" (pp. 155-156).

Civil society, as we have seen, has as its aim the adjudication of the system of needs. The state cannot be so seen. If the state is the embodiment of those various adjudications, then "it follows that membership in the state is something optional" (p. 156). The state requires unity. One cannot choose membership in ones state. (Hegel discusses exceptions to this which are consistent with his abhorrence of cosmopolitanism above.) Religion is a matter for the State to protect under the sphere of constitutional law but it must not be confused with the State. The State may notice public opinion but should never act on it. This follows Hegel's defense of a legislature. Democracy functions to the extent that officials are elected. Once elected, they should be allowed to carry out their duties. The procedures of the state itself are sufficiently strong to rid itself of "errant knights."

International law is the law governing autonomous states and their interactions with each other. Each state must see the other as possessing sovereign will. Indeed, states continue to recognize each other as states even while at war with one another.

World history is the culmination of right. "World-history is above the point of view from which these things matter. Each of its stages is the presence of a necessary moment in the Idea of the world mind, and that moment attains its absolute right in that stage" (p. 217). History follows the progression from the Oriental realm through the Greek and Roman realms to the Germanic realm. These realms are in strict hierarchical order for Hegel with the Germanic realm being the best. He ends his text,

> In the state, self-consciousness finds in an organic development the actuality of its substantive knowing and willing; in religion, it finds the feeling and the representation of this its own truth as an ideal essentiality; knowledge of this truth as one and the same in its mutually complementary manifestations, i.e. in the state, in nature, and in the ideal world (p. 222-223).

Having seen a text the dialectical reaction to Hegel may be seen more clearly in addition to the dialectical method at work in *Philosophy of Right*. This text so galled the young Karl Marx that he spent almost a year responding to it. Subsequent works, most notably the first volume of *Das Kapital* contain lengthy polemics against Hegel and his idealism, particularly as it is found in this work.

Still, Hegel describes the state as he found in ways that are very difficult to call into question. The state that he is describing was fearful of non-germanic persons and discriminatory of women. Seeing both the beauty of a structured state and its possibilities for evil has made many revolutionaries, many of whom call themselves dialecticians and who have their roots in their quarrels with Hegel.

Hegel casts a long shadow but perhaps not as long as his immediate predecessor, Immanuel Kant. In the next chapter we will examine Hegel's response to Kant.

3

Hegel's Answer to Kant

One cannot underestimate the importance of Kant and Hegel to twentieth century philosophy. True to his method, Hegel does not reject Kant outright; instead, he takes up those truths in epistemology, morality, and politics which accord with what is the case about the thinking world. Indeed in the political theory Hegel pays Kant high homage by having his *Philosophy of Right* follow the identical structure of Kant's *The Metaphysical Elements of Justice*. As we saw in the last chapter what is "the case about the world" is not going to be some rarefied view of what should be the case but what Hegel actually sees to the case. According to Hegel, Kant's magnificent edifice to human capacity, dignity, and value remained blind, on occasion, to the totality of experience. His answer to Kant is not a rejection of him but a continued conversation.

In an introduction to a philosopher who is sometimes referred to as a great theologian, as opposed to, or in addition to, being a great philosopher, we have not discussed God very much. Discussing both Kant and Hegel makes talk about God necessary. The concept of God is crucial to both systems and more similar in structural terms that might appear at first read. The systems share that they are shot through with God but they do not depend on God. Hegel's absolute spirit is often interpreted as God but whatever the concept Hegel has in mind it is not in accord with most conventional Christian views. For one thing, absolute spirit needs history to unfold for it to become conscious of itself. This dependence of a deity on human events puts a damper on the omnipotence traditionally assigned to God.

Kant's position is no less complicated although his view is consistent with the Pietist tradition, in which he finds himself. In that

38

tradition one takes seriously the scriptural injunctions against public discussion of inner religious experience and conviction. Thus, it makes sense that Kant would not discuss God in any but the most abstract terms.

Still, it is more complicated than this for Kant. Worried that in the moral realm a theory which does not have rational and independent justifications for its imperatives would be meaningless to empiricists, for example, who do not always believe in God, he felt forced to take God's rationality out of the foundation for theory. He writes:

> A metaphysics of morals is thus indispensably necessary, not merely because of motives of speculation regarding the source of practical principles which are present a priori in our reason, but because morals themselves are liable to all kinds of corruption as long as the guide and supreme norm for correctly estimating them are missing. For in the case of what is to be morally good, that it conforms to the moral law is not enough; it must be done for the sake of the moral law (*Grounding for the Metaphysics of Morals*, p. 3).

Kant is concerned that absent such a metaphysics of morals those who do not fear God would have no reason for knowing that what is right is right, what is wrong, wrong. Additionally, without the authority of God, there is no reason for people to follow paths of right action. More important philosophically for Kant, there is nothing but this metaphysics of morals which would fit both requirements: for the delineation of right acts and motivation for right action.

Empirical justifications for morality will always be subject to change and as such are only accidentally binding. Only practical principles grounded in pure reason must be seen as necessary to rational beings. For example, if the reason I am dutiful to my parents is because I expect an inheritance I may perform all the right actions. Such an ethic however is dangerous. Those whose parents have no estates have on that model no reason to treat their parents with respect. Allowing consequences of our actions to determine them undermines not only our own inner goodness but the fabric of society. One should honor one's parents simply and only because it is the right thing to do.

That both Hegel and Kant are concerned with God but do not use God per se as either foundation or telos puts their systems apart from most systems that precede them. There are philosophers preceding them who reject God outright. More commonly however are the philosophical systems which whenever stuck with not-knowing revert to the foundation of God's goodness—his unwillingness to trick us or deceive us.

In sum, for Kant, rationalizing those portions of God and specifically Christianity into the system, but keeping any foundation on God at bay, was a means of staving up skeptical arguments against him. Hegel makes God dependent on the system in a move that some call atheistic, others reduce to a kind of post-enlightenment pantheism, and still others view as the culmination of Protestant Christianity. However one reads God in these systems, it is not the God of earlier systems and it opened the space for from Kant's case, analytic philosophy and from Hegel's case existentialism, phenomenology, and ultimately, deconstruction.

In this century, it still remains roughly, if parochially true, that if one identifies as an analytic philosopher, one will be more Kantian than Hegelian. Indeed I once studied with an analytic philosopher who challenged me to find "just one argument" in Hegel's corpus. The Kantian streak often includes a kind of fierce anti-Hegelianism. Generally speaking those who find themselves favoring existentialism, phenomenology, or deconstruction spend more time dealing with Hegel. It is interesting, and perhaps a significant comment on Hegel's method, that very few of those identify as Hegelian. Whatever turns out to be the case, they end up engaging with Hegel more than their analytic counterparts.

After a brief overview of the two thinkers on the topics mentioned: epistemology, morality, and politics, we will revisit this schism within philosophy, and in the process learn more about Hegel.

Kant

It is sufficiently daunting to try to explain Hegel in such short space. To throw Kant into the mix really pushes the process over the top. Still, one cannot appreciate Hegel without looking at the structures Kant erected against what he considered the scandal of philosophy: that philosophers could not prove the existence of the external world. Kant was taken with the scientific revolution and was particularly interested with Copernicus' transformation of humanly lived reality. Booth explains this interest clearly:

Copernicus taught us that the sources of the planets' motion was to be sought in the observer. We also learned from him that man does not stand at the center of creation...The lessons of astronomy are many, Kant wrote, but its most important lesson is the revelation of the 'abyss of our ignorance', of how little we can know. The depth of our ignorance and our insignificance as natural beings is what we have learned from Copernicus. But in turning back our pretensions, the Copernican revolution directed reason to its true vocation to its 'ultimate purpose,' that is, to our affairs at the center of creation. So, too, Kant's rational theology taught us not to abandon 'the guidance of a morally legislative reason' in our actions for the sake of an ultimately fruitless search for knowledge of God and his commands

The 'startling consequence' is that *a priori* knowledge is possible, that the understanding is the law giver to nature but that beyond what can be given to us in possible experience, in the spatio-temporal framework of appearances governed by the categories, nothing can be known and what cannot not be known in the broad sense cannot be experienced (Booth, pp. 55-56).

The startling consequence, that *a priori* knowledge is possible is the result of an elaborate argument constructed to combat skepticism in general but most specifically the ingenious doubter, David Hume. Kant pretty much concedes that if one starts with empiricism, one ends with no possibility of certain knowledge claims. Kant will do for philosophy what Copernicus did for science: he will return the knowing subject to its center point and focus on the things which require attention of us from that vantage point.

Epistemology

Kant begins in a skeptical morass. Philosophy stood in need of a science which could determine the possibility, the principles, and the extent of all *a priori* knowledge. The aforementioned Hume had placed *a priori* knowledge beyond the realm of certainty. He argued that since there is no justifiable reason for supposing that we know propositions based on induction, this was proof that reason did not result in helping us justify even the most simple kinds of propositions. For example, he thought it to be the case that we could not affirm with certainty "I know that tomorrow the sun will rise."

Put philosophically the problem was: How are *a priori* synthetics judgments possible? How is metaphysics, as a natural disposition possible? How is metaphysics as science possible? Scientific knowledge is the purported result of the *Critique of Pure Reason*. Kant had conceded that to dogmatically employ reason, to do old-style metaphysics, is to make specious claims which claims can always be countered with skepticism. *A priori* statements are those which if known are known by reason alone: an *a priori* synthetic judgment is one made about the "real world" with its foundation in *a priori* statements. In contemporary terms what Kant was looking for were answers to these questions: How is it possible to make judgments about things and concepts which have mathematical certainty? How can our knowledge claims about our most basic assumptions carry the scientific force of scientific laws? How can I prove that a tree exists? How can I know that "right" and "wrong" have substantial and eternal meaning?

Kant thought that if we could prove that by the pure concepts of understanding alone, an object can be thought, we would be able to begin to answer the questions of the preceding paragraph. That is, he thought if we could make sense of an object using only pure concepts, this would prove the validity of the pure concepts. (We'd be able to affirm our knowledge in the sun rising as usual.) Using his terms, he thought that showing that the pure concepts alone allow for the thinking of an object is a sufficient deduction of them. That is, if they are necessary for the thinking of an object, they exist necessarily. Not only that, that showing will justify the subjective sources in their transcendental constitution which form the *a priori* foundation of the possibility of experience.

Another way to put this is that if it can be proved that the pure concepts of understanding are sufficient grounding for me to say "I know that this is a table" then the "I" of that sentence and the concepts I use to utter that judgment, are necessary, *a priori* grounding that experience is possible. This move, if it works, successfully counters the skeptic who asks "How can I know with certainty that the table is real?" Kant's answer would erase the question as necessarily absurd, that is devoid of sense and meaning.

The deduction of the pure concepts looks like this:

1. The possibility of combination in general—that objects can only be understood insofar as the subject has represented them in a certain way to itself—shows that the subject combines objects. Example: objects don't appear as three dimensional—we make them that way. It must be possible that they are three dimensional. This is an act of synthesis that cannot be denied.

2. The original synthetic unity of apperception is similarly undeniable. It must be possible for the I-think to accompany all representations else sense is impossible. For this to be possible, and it must be possible, the I-think must be unified

and it must be original. Synthesis and the transcendental unity of apperception make it possible to understand representations: "Otherwise it would be possible for appearances to crowd in upon the soul, and yet to be such as would never allow of experience. Since connection in accordance with universal and necessary laws would be lacking, all relation of knowledge to objects would fall away" *Critique of Pure Reason*, p. 138).

3. The principle of the synthetic unity is the supreme principle of all employment of the understanding. It is an objective condition of knowledge.

4. The objective unity of self-consciousness is different from the subjective unity of consciousness. We may often feel as if we have objective unity of consciousness when in fact it is merely subjective. There is a difference between the two therefore the objective unity must exist for us to "feel" it subjectively. That is, there is a difference between something appearing truly or falsely to me and something that is the case. The I-think often gets it right. Therefore, it is absurd to deny the difference.

5. The logical form of all judgments consists in the objective unity of the apperception of the concepts which they contain. Kant writes: "a judgment is nothing but the manner in which given modes of knowledge are brought to the objective unity of apperception. This is what is intended by the copula is...It indicates their relation to original apperception, and its *necessary unity*. It holds good even if the judgment is itself empirical, and therefore contingent, as, for example, in the judgment, 'Bodies are heavy.' I do not here assert that these representations necessarily belong to one another in the empirical intuition, but that they belong to one another in virtue of the necessary unity of apperception in the synthesis of intuitions, that is, according to principles of objective determination of all representation...Thus to say 'the body is heavy' is not merely to state that the two representations have always been conjoined in my perception, however often that perception be repeated; what we are asserting is that they are combined in the object no matter what the state of the subject may be" (*Critique of Pure Reason*, p. 159).

6. But this (the necessary unity of apperception in synthesis) is possible only under categories independent from the subject. Therefore there must be categories. There could be no empirical knowledge without the categories.

7. "The deduction is the exposition of the pure concepts of the understanding, and therewith of all theoretical *a priori* knowledge, as principles of the possibility of experience—the principles being here taken as the determination of appearances in space and time in general and this determination, in turn, as ultimately following from the original synthetic unity of apperception, as the form of the understanding in its relation to space and time, the original forms of sensibility" (*Critique of Pure Reason*, p. 175).

Kant has argued that the things we experience would make no sense at all if skepticism were true. That is, if we were never certain of what appears to us, nothing could mean anything. But things mostly make sense. We navigate the world with astonishing accuracy. We impose pure concepts over things in a systematic way so things, rational beings, and concepts exist and they exist necessarily because our experience of them mostly makes sense.

Furthermore, it is simultaneously the case that these things are related structurally by affinity. The synthetic unity of apperception is as necessary to possible experience as is the integrity of objects. Kant shifts the epistemological burden to the other side. If someone wants to worry about the underlying reality of our sense perceptions, Kant wants a coherent narrative, even better would be an argument, as to why the worry should be taken seriously.

Morality

For Kant, when a person acts that person is acting on some sort of general principle whether the principle is known to the person or not. According to him there are two universal laws. The universal law of nature which describes how things must be. The universal law of freedom describes how all people ought to act in a certain set of circumstances. For Kant we are capable of willing states of affairs that we can simultaneously will as universal laws. A contradictory willing is one such that a person can be said to will contradictorily if s/he wills that p be the case, and that q be the case, and that it is impossible that p and q both be the case. For example, when a person tells a lie that person is acting on a principle that it is permissible to lie. This is contradictory because one cannot consistently will this permission. One is always willing the principle of truth in order that language means what it says, etc. It is a necessary contradiction in anyone's willing that this eternal wiling be thwarted by the will to lie.

In both morality and epistemology the appearance of things and their underlying reality become important. Notice in the paragraph above that persons act under certain laws whether they know this or not. Kant describes us as being both phenomenal (apparent) and noumenal (real) selves. (Some interpreters argue that this claim in Kant is an ontological one. That is, they believe that Kant's position is that we *are* two selves. I side with those who believe that he is describing two ways we experience ourselves.) One's phenomenal self has things appear to it that are known as experience according to the argument outlined above. There remains an unknown because we cannot know or directly experience our noumenal selves. We only know of them that they must exist. If they did not, then the aforementioned absurdities would ensue. That is, if we imagine the possibility of only the phenomenal self existing, "principles" and objects would appear helter skelter with nothing to hold them fast. As the representations of objects appeared to us we would have no faculty "telling" us what to pay attention to. It would just be indistinguishable shapes, colors, light rushing toward us.

In the realm of morality this distinction is peculiarly important because the root of skepticism is our uncertainty about whether an action is right. For Kant we can know what the right thing is (the right thing is that which can be willed consistently by rational things), we can know that we are bound to do it (we have an affinity with reason, failing to act in accord to is contradicting our nature), and we can know whether we do the right thing (does this action accord with the right thing?). What we can never know is if we are acting according to duty or simply out of self-interest. That is the pure concepts of the understanding are grounding for the three things we know. There is no similarly accessible mechanism for understanding whether we are good. The good will acts simply because it is the right thing to do. But we do not always operate according to the good will, more is the pity. Therefore, in any given case, our motives will be opaque to us. We cannot know whether our will is good. For example, if I tell the truth it could be because I do not want to incur the wrath of my friend. This is not the reason to tell the truth. If this were my reason, I would be free to lie were I unfortunate enough to have friends who do not care about my honesty nor our mutual trust.

Some commentators believe that the opacity of the good will is necessary to maintaining a consistent theology. Were we to have access to the goodness or badness of our will, then we would be in a position to judge our moral worthiness. We are commanded to view all rational beings as infinitely morally worthy. Only God is allowed to make judgments of degree. To return to the case of respecting one's parents. I could tell myself that I honor my parents because that is what a good daughter does. Still, there is a part of me that might perform the actions of filial piety with an eye on the inheritance. This struggle over my own motivations can only be decided, according to Kant, by a Being that has access to all knowledge. (This point is belabored because as we have seen Hegel supposes himself to be that kind of Being.)

Skepticism is answered by the distinction between noumenal and phenomenal objects, including our selves. Skeptics thought that they did not know what was right; what they in fact did not know is whether they were acting rightly. In the theory of knowledge the certainty that things appear to us in mostly consistent fashion proves that there is an underlying reality, the world of noumenal objects. In morality, the results of that certainly allow the knowledge that what Kant calls the categorical imperative carries absolute necessity. And as Kant says ,

> Everyone must admit that if a law is to be morally valid, i.e., is to be valid as a ground of obligation, then it must carry with it absolute necessity. He must admit that the command, 'Thou shalt not lie,' does not hold only for men, as if other rational beings had no need to abide by it, and so with all the other moral laws properly so called. And he must concede that the ground of obligation here must not be sought in the nature of man nor in the circumstances of the world in which man is placed, but must be sought a priori solely in the concepts of pure reason (*Grounding for the Metaphysics of Morals,* p, 2).

The categorical imperative is the formal principle by which all practical rules are derived and reads in its first formulation: "Hence there is only one categorical imperative and it is this: Act only according to that maxim whereby you can at the same time will that it should become a universal law" (*Grounding for the Metaphysics of Morals,* p. 30).

Political Theory

Given what we have seen with respect to Kant's theories of knowledge and morality, the political theory offers few surprises. He argues:

> In the practical exercise of reason, however, the concept of freedom proves its reality through practical basic principles. As laws of a causality of pure reason, these principles determine the

will independently of all empirical conditions (independently of anything sensible) and prove the existence in us of a pure Will in which moral concepts and laws have their origin.

On this concept of freedom, which is positive (from a practical point of view), are founded unconditional practical laws which are called *moral* (*The Metaphysical Elements of Justice*, p. 22).

This passage shows that for Kant, freedom is inherent in persons. Law and morality flow from this inherent freedom and we are said to have natural rights with attendant obligations. States, for Kant, can turn out to be wrong. Their validity is not determined by historical context; instead it is determined by moral absolutes, as defined above.

Kant does not see morality in a logically distinct sphere from justice. Indeed justice must be moral. The definition of freedom with which he operates is (1) that it is a pure concept of reason, (2) that it is transcendent, noumenal, and hence not knowable but it is ontologically provable by means of a transcendental argument, and (3) it only acts in accordance with necessity. A person for Kant "is the subject whose actions are susceptible to imputation. Accordingly, moral personality is nothing but the freedom of a rational being under moral laws" (*The Metaphysical Elements of Justice*, p. 24). For Kant, each persons wills only for him or herself.

The realm of justice covers external practical interrelationships, the will to will interrelationships, and the form of will. Justice is the aggregate of those conditions under which the will of one person can be conjoined with the will of another in accordance with universal freedom. For Kant, then, the universal principle of justice becomes:

> Every action is just that in itself or in its maxim is such that the freedom of the will of each con coexist with the freedom of everyone in accordance with a universal law (*The Metaphysical Elements of Justice*, p. 35).

Some of the duties which befall political beings are to be honorable, to do no one an injustice (when one is not sure whether one is about to commit an injustice, one should make an autonomous exit from society for as long as takes—a sort of self-imposed, grown-up time-out), and to be responsible for your duties. Kant argues that propositions about rights can be synthetic *a priori* and that consequently, right can be understood analytically.

For Kant, as for Hegel, private law involves property. But for Kant one has an obligation to *choose* to be in a State from what would still be the private sphere. Public law, by contrast, involves constitutional law and legislative bodies and execution. For Kant, the well-being of the State is not reducible to the well-being of the citizens. One judges the well-being of a state by analyzing how closely its constitution conforms to the Categorical Imperative. Even in states-craft Kant remains staunchly anti-consequentialist. As in the moral theory, Kant is concerned that we remember that we will always know what is right and that we can do the right thing. (This is analytic, we cannot be obliged to do what we cannot do.) Problems arise when we let consequences sully the only proper motive, that we do the right thing because it is the right thing.

Kant does not use terms like "world history;" still he recognizes international law, believing that if states act justly and respect each other's autonomy, then there is a possibility of perpetual peace. To accomplish this one must move from a hostile view of nature to one from which one recognizes one's freedom is only to be found in the recognition of nature's goodness. Shell describes the process well. She writes:

> Kant set himself the difficult task of recovering and reasserting the spiritual assurances which science seemed irrevocably to destroy...We perceive nature not only as hostile but also as unjust, and we claim a right to the satisfaction which nature denies us. By itself this claim cannot alleviate our troubles. In venting our anger against the world we rail against necessity. But our indignation can deliver us if we direct it inward against ourselves. Such self-opposition makes possible self-overcoming or the transcendence of nature within us. Kant's final response to the human predicament is an assertion of the rights of man and of the power these rights confer to transcend in freedom and in dignity the natural world of which man is a conditioned and inconsequential part...With the redirection of anger, man becomes not only as asserter of claims but also a possessor of rights (Shell, p. 42).

As we shall see the role of nature will occasion vigorous disagreement from Hegel on everything from property to family to statehood and its status. Hegel describing states as they occur could hardly hold them to anything so lofty as the Categorical Imperative. He could not disagree more with Kant's statement that "the guarantee of perpetual peace is nothing less than that great artist, nature (*natura daedala rerum)"* (*Perpetual Peace,* p. 24). Not only is peace not an aim one can pose, it certainly could not be guaranteed by nature. The difference in their positions first arises at the level of the possible knowledge of things.

Hegel

Hegel is fierce in his desire to keep the subject an object of knowledge without reducing it to a thing. It is in elaborating this desire that he founds modern phenomenology which has among many other contributions the following theses to commend itself. First, it unabashedly affirms that objects are. We may as well start there. Second, it sees subjects on equal ontological footing to objects although subjects differ from objects in the character of their conscious and unconscious intentionality. An overview of Hegel's epistemology viewed as a response to Kant will clarify these issues.

Epistemology

Contrast what we saw in Kant's deduction with Hegel's blunt claim that "But the object *is:* it is what is true, or it is the essence. It is, regardless of whether it is known or not; and it remains, even if it is not known, whereas there is no knowledge if the object is not there" (*Phenomenology*, 93, p. 59). This may seem to indicate a more blunt position than is the case. Remember that for Hegel everything must be qualified with respect to its position in system and its historical introduction into spirit. What is the case about objects and subjects in the stage of e.g. sense certainty is not the only case. Kolb elaborates:

> For Hegel, nothing is immediate, in thought or in actuality. Thought and its relation to reality must be thought in terms of the motion of the absolute form: universality (the logic), particularity (the logical categories spread out in otherness in nature), individuality (the logical categories as forming self-aware individuals, spirit). Each of these moments exists through the others; no one moment is 'first' (Kolb, p. 86).

Hegel's totality, the contextualized but simultaneous occurrence of the three modes precludes questions about what is the noumenal? What is the thing in itself? That is, Kant's positing of things in themselves as a necessary condition of the foundation of knowledge is not necessary to Hegel's way of philosophical thinking. He recognizes that Kantian theory is an advance over preceding theories. Still, Hegel is dissatisfied with not being able to know an underlying reality. The bridge from things as they appear to things as they are in fact can be viewed as metaphorical, if, but only if, it is a universal condition of the fact of our knowing. As such, it might be able to be brought up into an ideal progression of knowledge in a world where we acknowledge that there is only one thing and it is consciousness.

This move staves off questions of how to cross the bridge. Kolb is helpful yet again. He writes,

> For Hegel, banning such questions is an important move beyond Kant, who surrounded his deduction of the categories with a story about things in themselves. The absolute form of the motion of the concept and idea provides its own space within itself for any transitions and application that must be made.
>
> When the logical sequence is thought through according to its own pattern, the whole contents of the world and self-consciousness are included, at least in their necessary aspects. There is no application of the completed categorical sequence to a foreign realm. This relentless extension of encompassing unity is meant to forestall questions of the kind we usually ask about causes and mechanism. There is no change or transition which requires an external cause; we are thinking the necessary structure of the whole within which we find ourselves by thinking the necessary structure of pure thought. For Hegel, our yearning for explanatory mechanisms reflects a failure to understand how the logical categories are more fundamental than any explanation we could give of their transition to nature and spirit (Kolb, pp. 86-87).

So fundamental, in fact, that calling them into question reveals a topsy-turvy world where that one not-knowing suspends knowledge of the most important kind for Hegel—the knowledge of universals. Zizek explains while discussing Kant:

> ...as soon as the Thing-in-itself is posited as unattainable, *every universal is potentially suspended.* Every universal implies a point of exception at which its validity, its hold, is canceled; or, to put it in the language of contemporary physics, it implies a point of singularity. This 'singularity' is ultimately *the Kantian subject himself,* namely the empty subject of the transcendental apperception (Zizek, p. 45).

The subject in Kant knows from a formal standpoint and is formal itself. Hegel wants to capture this tension, of the suspended universal and the formal subject, in his phenomenology of spirit and wonders what would happen if we collapse noumena and phenomena. If there were just the one thing, idea, how would a subject retain that tension of an other outside of itself? If there were just the one thing, idea, how would anything move beyond its own identity. His answer is that self-consciousness is always already reflected by its own doubling and by the self-consciousnesses which surround it. Zizek writes:

> This original doubling of self-consciousness provides the foundation of 'intersubjectivity': if, as the Hegelian commonplace goes, self-consciousness is self-consciousness only through the mediation of another self-consciousness, then my self-awareness—precisely insofar as this self-awareness is not the same as self-transparency—causes the emergence of a decentered 'it thinks' (Zizek, p. 68).

Hegel's subject is able to know and is not even really interested in skepticism except as a stage through which it goes on its way to understanding itself as completely in the world. Any given subjectivity must encounter and reject skepticism as absolute spirit encountered and rejected skepticism on its way to absolute knowledge.

> What we have prior the Kantian subject is not the intersubjectivity proper but a community of individuals who share a common universal-substantial ground and participate in it. It is only with Kant, with his notion of the subject as ~(S), as the empty form of self-apperception, as an entity which constitutively 'does not know what it is,' that the Other Subject is needed in order for me to define my own identity: what the Other thinks I am is inscribed into the very heart of my own most intimate self-identity (Zizek, pp. 68-69).

The subject is no longer isolated from things or other subjects. It is part of the world as knower and as thing known. The empty, not-a-subject of Kantian epistemology needs to be mirrored to know itself. The Hegelian subject is only in a subject in the presence of other subjects. One cannot make sense of a sole Hegelian subject. In epistemology what this means is that Hegelian subjectivity implies the rejection of eternal universals except the absolute principle of identity.

But even this principle "slides." Zizek shows that the principle of identity is always on the verge of exceeding itself. For Hegel,

> In short, identity hinges on what makes a difference. We pass from identity to difference the moment we grasp that the 'identity' of an entity consists of the cluster of its differential features. The social identity of person X, for example, is composed of the cluster of its social mandates which are all by definition differential: a person is 'father' only in relation to 'mother' and 'son'; in another relation, he is himself 'son,' etc. (Zizek, p. 130).

So epistemology gets all tied up in both morality and if not full blown political theory at least ethical life. The shift toward a philosophy that deals with its various branches simultaneously is sometimes viewed as a reversion to Greek philosophy. I hope that the excursion to this point through Kant goes some way to dispelling this view. To be sure Plato sees theories of knowledge and morality as tightly linked but this is largely because he argues that if one knows the truth one will necessarily be good. Hegel does not contradict this view for absolute spirit. Pertaining to that view he holds as many positions as he addresses historical epochs and social formations. Thus many people act contrary to the truths they know and Hegel gives examples. Furthermore, for Hegel, the point is not in connecting empty concepts formally but in elaborating ideas in their varied interconnectedness.

Morality

As we have seen morality's place is between abstract right and ethical life. That is to say that abstract right (the right for each individual in him or herself) is superceded by morality, the realm of freedom, which in turn is superceded by ethical life. Morality is that which has to do with the subject, i.e., the being that is self-consciously a willing being. In the moral sphere the principle is that of the infinite subjectivity of freedom. This is to say that in morality the will now has for its objects the personality. There is a movement from the will of abstract right to that of morality described by Hegel as the negation of the negation. First the will is in opposition between its implicit universal will and its own explicitly independent will. By negating the negation of the two opposing wills, the will determines itself in its existence as a will. The will is no longer just in-itself but for-itself.

Morality is superceded by ethical (social) life for Hegel but not for Kant. Thus for instance, the domain of family and its attendant contracts and responsibilities is not the realm of morality for Hegel. The individual free will for itself is subsumed by this the first social unity. Kant however does not have the notion of a universal law outside of the willing individual. Thus, Kant's realm of morality maintains the individual in morality because the universal law is one with the universal law giver. So, for example, marriage is an ethical issue for Hegel and a moral issue for Kant. The right pertaining to groupings of human beings, the family, etc., belongs to the metaphysical elements of justice for Kant. Hegel rejects this notion, i.e., that legislation can be that which pertains to the individuals in their relations to each other.

Another example of divergence is found in Hegel's analysis of the system of needs in civil society. Because civil society is the battlefield of interests (competing and individual ones) the right attaching to civil society cannot be with relation to each individual. It must be the synthesis of those competing needs. Kant's notion of the autonomy of the individual persisting through civil society cannot allow morality to be superceded at this early point. Kojeve has argued that the autonomy of the individual through the moral sphere overlooks the fact that there are necessarily contradictions in society. He might argue that Kant's theory does not account for the reality of conflict whereas Hegel's system is in fact descriptive of a reality replete with contradiction.

A concise account of Hegel's critique of Kant is given here:

> Kant's moral cosmology is 'a nest of thoughtless contradictions'...Consciousness jumps from position to position around a circle, without maintaining any of them seriously. The starting position is that there is actual moral consciousness in the natural world. But when the agent acts, the harmony is realized, so the postulate is not needed (Harris, p. 75).

For Hegel, that the moral consciousness exists as original in the natural world doesn't make a lot of sense. He is concerned with action more than anything else and only at the point of action can we begin to determine the rightness or wrongness of actions. (This does not mean that Hegel doesn't think we should think about moral principles. They simply cannot arise until there have been a critical mass of actions. By that point we are already not in the "natural world. This general divergence does not reduced Hegel to the merely consequentialist position that Kant derides. It may well however reduce him to the anthropology of morals Kant also derides—where one reads what is moral by observing the actions of, necessarily imperfect, human beings. Still, Kantians may want to answer the question about action Hegel poses so skillfully. I agree with Westphal that:

> No contemporary attempt to develop a theory of morality in the Kantian tradition would be responsible if it ignored the Hegelian critique of Kantian ethics. At the center of that critique is the claim that the principles and maxims of pure practical reason are insufficiently specific to give definite answers to basic moral questions arising in everyday life (Westphal, p. 55).

The criticism of morality is not without ramification for the political theory. If morality and political theory have basically the same logical principles under which they must operate, and those principles cannot attend to context, it is hard to make sense of the everyday sorts of problems we encounter. For instance is my relation to my daughter different in kind than that to my nieces? Is a nation's president subject to different morality than the citizens he serves? Does a good leader need to suspend the principles of morality, but never of ethics, to maintain power for citizens of her country? Kant is admirable in his consistency of principle and his delicacy of explanation. He deals with all these cases with responses ranging from different principles apply because of the maxims which describe the action to sometimes we have to choose to do the wrong thing knowing that we are doing the wrong thing. Hegel is more pragmatic than that. Westphal is helpful yet again:

> Though the rhetoric of Hegel's critique of Kant sometimes suggests that he takes Kant's principle to be completely empty, a more charitable and philosophically fruitful reading would be something like this: by seeking to ground morality on a reason which abstracts from historical-social conditioning, Kant can only produce a principle which is manifestly too empty. Human ethical life requires more specific guidance (Westphal, pp. 60-61).

Political Theory

It is short work to finish the differences by focusing on political theory. Hegel follows the structure of Kant's work, as mentioned earlier, so the interested student can sit down with both books and look at their disagreements. (It is interesting that Kant the sterner with respect to absolute principles comes off as kinder but I leave the agreement of that judgment to the interested reader.) Jacobson sums up the general differences well:

> Hegel's criticism of Kant is twofold. First a jurisprudence of duty cannot be founded on rational premises. Only a jurisprudence of right can, and only according to a different criterion of rationality than universal legislation. Second, Hegel's answer to the question, Why should I perform my duties?, is that you love the person to whom you owe the duty, not that you wish to be rational (Jacobson, p. 111).

The first criticism shows how deep the difference between the two is. Abstract right can be based solely on the abstract principles of reason but only a reason that recognizes itself as based on Logic as Hegel as described it—an almost living thing. Duty just cannot be based on reason for Hegel. The conversation Kant and Hegel have about marriage is interesting in this regard. The reader will recall that Kant believes marriage to be a contract while Hegel abhors this idea. In our examples about motivation when discussing Kant we used only bad motivations. Kant also eschews good ones if they are not those for love of duty alone. When teaching Kant students always raise the point that they do not want their, usually future, children to treat them well out of duty but because they do love them and they want them to be happy. I tell them that they have anticipated Hegel's argument as indeed they have.

These differences so concisely captured by Jacobson point to important divergences. For instance when Hegel talks about international law the furthest thing from his mind is the possibility of peace. He starts "knowing" that we can aim for the fullest expression of our states but that this will include strife—just as our interior lives include tension and our logic includes contradiction. If one responds that surely it is better to at least envision the possibility of the world according to Kant since only someone irrational could favor war over peace then one is not talking to Hegel at all. The place from which one rationally favors peace over war is not the place humans get to be. In this conflict at this time, we prefer that it be over but it is contrary to experience to state the position as Kant does. This does not mean that Hegel loves conflict only that he expects conflict. The point is of course not minor. It is at points such as these that one notices the danger of philosophy in general. Most philosophers have been more on Hegel's side than Kant's. Plato sees the inevitability of war as being tied to our desire for having more luxuries than our neighbor. Hegel is dangerous precisely because he puts his pronouncements outside of prescription. When we come to Hegel's critics we will explore further the notion that while utopian thought has its share of producing pain in history, *realpolitik* is not immune from bad consequences.

4

The Philosopher's Role in the Analysis of Culture

Hegelian Culture

By culture (*Bildung*) Hegel means something quite specific. He means the normal things one does when specifying things cultural: economic institutions, the arts, religion, the letters, and the social milieu in general. He additionally assigns it a special role both in world history and also in the logical space of what might be called the social. World historically, culture is the stage of the Enlightenment. During this time period, for Hegel, there was a deep alienation of spirit from itself because the dominant ideology of the day told a story to individuals about themselves that did not quite make sense to them. They "were told" that they carried the law of both morality and right within them. Consequently, there was a rift between the person's sense of him or herself, the picture painted by dominant discourse, and the reality experienced through religion, state and revolution.

For instance, during the Enlightenment there were two opposite poles of "absolute value." On the one hand, a reverence for utility whatever the cost and on the other, an evolving though initially superstitious relationship to religion. Language becomes especially important here because it must find a way to speak contradictions as if they were part of a unified truth. The force of that language does bring about a kind of unity as we shall see.

The Philosopher's Role in the Analysis of Culture

Spirit is confused at the point of culture: nothing is as it seems to be:

> It is this absolute and universal inversion and alienation of the actual world and of thought; it is *pure culture*. What is learnt in this world is that neither the *actuality* of power and wealth, nor their specific Notions, 'good' and 'bad', or the consciousness of 'good' and 'bad', possess truth; on the contrary, all these moments become inverted, one changing into the other, and each is the opposite of itself (*Phenomenology of Spirit*, 521, p. 316).

During this phase of spirit it fancies itself charming and witty when it is pandering most shamelessly to whatever is best regarded by the persons surrounding it. The record of the time will be a distortion of the actuality because Spirit believes itself to be noble and powerful.

> The content of what Spirit says about itself is thus the perversion of every Notion and reality, the universal deception of itself and others; and the shamelessness which gives utterance to this deception is just for this reason the greatest truth (*Phenomenology of Spirit*, 522, p. 317).

Spirit itself is in pretty sorry shape but the persons living through it are worse. Hegel almost rises to the level of humor:

> It is the self-centered self that knows, not only how to pass judgment on and chatter about everything, but how to give witty expression to the *contradiction* that is present in the solid elements of the *actual* world, as also in the fixed determinations posited by judgment; and this contradiction is their truth. Looked at from the point of view of form, it knows everything to be self-alienated, being-for-self is separated from being-in-itself; what is meant, and purpose, are separated from truth; and from both again, the being-for-another, the ostensible meaning from the real meaning, from the true thing and intention. Thus it knows how to give correct expression to each moment in relation to its opposite, in general, how to express accurately the perversion of everything; it knows better than each what each is, no matter what its specific nature is. (*Phenomenology of Spirit*, 526, p. 320).

Spirit is finding its way to increased consciousness of itself and adolescent-like must devalue everything that appears to have value for others and to assert at each moment that it knows more about what is the case than those closest to the issues. (Spirit is telling persons with faith during this time that they don't know their true self which is the self in which abstract justice inheres.)

In terms of the logic of subjective development, culture is the time during which we do not know who we are with respect to the cultural markers which parade themselves as true markers. With sufficient shaking up of categories, we will proceed to morality where we once again know who we are, only this time we know who we are with a knowledge of the extent of our capacity for vanity. We will also know what with certainty whereas before we knew only from self-alienation. But this shaking up of self awareness, which in terms of personal development might have had as its most serious consequences having embarrassed oneself, or ones parents too many times at dinner parties, for Spirit itself the result of the shake up will be a reign of terror.

The structure of Culture for Hegel is as follows. Culture is the middle term between true spirit, which is the ethical order and spirit that is certain of itself, in this case morality. Spirit in between these two stages is self-alienated spirit. The world of self-alienated spirit contains culture and its realm of actuality and religion (in its unrevealed form). The Enlightenment arises because religion has remained "essentially merely a *belief*" (*Phenomenology*, 528, p. 322). Pure insight is called up to counter the disappointment in recognizing that one is living in mere belief. This disappointment leads one to look for a stronger sense of oneself and ones roles in culture. The result is a heightened faith which while living in culture allows for the ability to transcend culture and its vanity for real representations and understanding of the deity. That is, superstitious faith in mere picture-thinking is replaced by a pure insight of the deity and its role in culture. Still, pure insight is the not the same of religious faith and carries within it the detritus of the cultural malaise just described. Pure insight does not impel one to religious community, nor to morality; instead, it leads to enlightenment.

The argument is best left to Hegel who writes:

> Genius, talent, special capacities generally, belong to the world of actuality, in so far as this world still contains the aspect of being a spiritual animal kingdom in which individuals, amid confusion and mutual violence, cheat and struggle over the essence of the actual world. These

differences, it is true, have no place in this world as honest *especes;* individuality neither is contented with the unreal 'matter in hand' itself nor has it a *particular* content and ends of its own. On the contrary, it counts merely as something universally acknowledged, viz. as an educated individuality; and the difference is reduced to one of less or more energy, a *quantitative* difference...This last difference, however, ha been effaced by the fact that in the completely disrupted state of consciousness difference changed round into an absolutely qualitative difference. There, what is for the 'I' an 'other' is only the 'I' itself. In this infinite judgment all one-sidedness and peculiarity of the original being-for-self has been eradicated; the self knows itself *qua* pure self to be its own object; and this absolute identity of the two sides is the element of pure insight...This pure insight is thus the Spirit that calls to every consciousness: *be for yourselves* what you all are *in yourselves—reasonable* (*Phenomenology of Spirit,* 537, pp. 327-328).

In chapter two when discussing Kant and Hegel on God, I mentioned that Kant, that seminal Enlightenment figure, had banished God from the formal structure of his system for pedagogical as well as religious reasons. Hegel is not speaking directly to Kant here but he may as well be. He is arguing that the precepts of faith without the religious content, without God, are not left unscathed. Each step toward absolute knowledge is a step forward and the march through culture is as progressive as any other. Still, the supersession of simple faith in God for pure intuition has a very high cultural price. Indeed, there is a coldness in the Godless system that leaves out the very thing that Kant had wanted to save: moral motivation. Pure insight is opposed to what it sees as the perversion of culture (by which is only meant here the tendency to misrepresent things) and it is opposed to religious sentiment. Thus the Enlightenment, founded on pure insight is doomed to require a large dose of negation to get it to the next stage. The period of the Enlightenment has two moments: that of its struggle with superstition and that with its truth.

Hegel's prose is most colorful during this section as here is where Spirit sneaks up on someone so uncultured as to be involved with religious idols:

> Being now an invisible and imperceptible Spirit, it infiltrates the noble parts through and through and soon has taken

60

complete possession of all the vitals and members of the unconscious idol; then 'one fine morning it gives its comrade a shove with the elbow, and bang! crash! the idol lies on the floor' On 'one fine morning' whose noon is bloodless if the infection has penetrated to every organ of spiritual life (*Phenomenology*, 546, p. 332).

Continuing its fight against religious faith, the Enlightenment does not notice that it fails to accord rights in the manner in which it assigns them.

Further, Enlightenment maintains against the believer a right which the latter himself concedes, when Enlightenment regards the object of the believer's veneration as stone or wood, or else as something finite and anthropomorphic (*Phenomenology*, 578, p. 346.

There is truth in the enlightenment and that is the bringing together of utility and pure insight. "What is thus lacking is obtained in Utility in so far as pure insight there acquires positive objectivity; pure insight is thereby an actual consciousness satisfied within itself" (*Phenomenology*, 581, p. 355). The rationalists are overjoyed at the ability to be rationally religious, religiously mercantile, and take care of the troubles that confront them (often crushing poverty) without feeling the sting of either religious conscience or that of civil society: "The two worlds are reconciled and heaven is transplanted to earth below" (*Phenomenology*, 581, p. 355).

Heaven lasts for only a short time on earth. One of the doctrines of the enlightenment is that of absolute freedom. When "Consciousness has found its Notion in Utility" (*Phenomenology*, 582, p. 355), there is nothing that prohibits from any class of actions: "In this absolute freedom, therefore, all social groups or classes which are the spiritual spheres into which the whole is articulated are abolished" (*Phenomenology*, 585, p. 357). There can be neither special privilege nor special obligation attached to any social group. One has no reason to "know one's place," and if one cannot forget there is no reason to act on the knowledge. For Hegel, this is the breakdown of the possibility of anything positive: dialogue, work, mediation, etc. Instead this leads to the point where there is only negativity:

This movement is thus the interaction of consciousness with itself in which it lets nothing break loose to become a *free*

61

object standing over against it. It follows from this that it cannot achieve anything positive, either universal works of language or of reality, either of laws and general institutions of *conscious* freedom, or of deeds and works of a freedom that *wills* them (*Phenomenology*, 588, p. 358).

All this energy could proceed somewhere, one supposes, but for Hegel, the energy ultimately ends is rage: "Universal freedom, therefore, can produce neither a positive work nor a deed; there is left for it only *negative* action; it is merely the *fury* of destruction (*Phenomenology*, 589, p. 359). Fury of this magnitude with neither inner nor cultural check produces terror:

> The sole work and deed of universal freedom is therefore death, a death too which has no inner significance or filling, for what is negated is the empty point of the absolutely free self. It is thus the coldest and meanest of all deaths, with no more significance than cutting off a head of cabbage or swallowing a mouthful of water (*Phenomenology*, 591, p. 360).

Once the point of terror has been reached, Spirit quickly looks for its development of moral qualities. It passes over into that next sphere:

> The culture to which it attains in interaction with that essence is, therefore, the grandest and the last, is that of seeing its pure, simple reality immediately vanish and pass away into empty nothingness. In the world of culture itself it does not get as far as to behold its negation or alienation in this form of pure abstraction; on the contrary, its negation is filled with a content, either honour or wealth, which it gains in place of the self in absolute freedom; its negation is the death that is without meaning, the sheer terror of the negative that contains nothing positive, nothing that fills it with content"(*Phenomenology*, 594, p. 362).

The description of culture is a puzzling one. A simple reading would lead one to believe that Hegel might think that times of heavy cultural productivity lead to sheer negativity. He clearly does not think that. One could imagine instead that Hegel is trying to find a way to most clearly point out that there is a direct relationship between the kinds of cultural products we revere and the social and political states we either endure, justifiably support, or actively seek to dismantle. It seems clear that Hegel believes that the thinkers of the Enlightenment have responsibility for the way in which the reign of terror worked itself out. But he is in a bit of a pickle. He is a Wise Man telling the story of absolute spirit. He can hardly be expected to comment on the state of the theater in his neighborhood. I think that we can find out very interesting things about Hegel by paying attention to the places where he plays the role of analyzer of culture and where he does not. It appears that where the role of analysis slows down the completion of history, he is going to remain largely silent.

Hegel's Relationship to Culture

In the section we have just examined, Hegel is probably referring to Kant and Adam Smith among others. He is also making reference to the institutions of culture which would include in addition to social classes and their acoutrements, music, dance, theater, and letters. He refers to only one work by name in the entire section. (Diderot's *Rameau's Nephew*.) This is an interesting fact and one that shows that the first relation Hegel has to culture is universal as opposed to particular. He is less interested in any particular cultural artifact than in the sum total of how those cultural artifacts mirror reality. We could ask ourselves what is more important about movies today—an in depth analysis of *Pokemon* or a discussion which does not refer to it but discusses the making-consumer of children through films that have reached a point where the dialogue is not merely empty chatter to wrap around the products, but is just the toys for purchase repeating their names over and over again?

The astute reader will perhaps be annoyed at the example because there is no in-depth account possibly forthcoming about the work referred to above. (What would it mean to write or speak that account?) In a sense it doesn't matter what the work is, in discussing this relation. What is clear is that not only could one produce an in-depth analysis of culture with reference to *Pokemon* one could do so without watching the movie.

Hegel refers in his lectures on aesthetics only rarely to works and then to ones everyone will know. These references are in passing, as for instance when he remarks

> Tieck no doubt always says there ought to be Irony; but when he himself approaches the criticism of great works of art, though his recognition and portrayal of their greatness is excellent, yet, if we fancy that now is the best opportunity to

explain where the Irony is. e.g. in such a work as *Romeo and Juliet,* we are taken in—for we hear no more about the Irony (*Introductory Lectures on Aesthetics,* p. 75).

In addition to being concerned with the universal movement of culture as opposed to its discrete parts, Hegel is concerned with the manner in which culture impacts other areas of consciousness coming to know itself. Thus, the writings in the realm of aesthetics deal almost exclusively with other philosophers of aesthetics.

Finally Hegel is far more concerned with what the art represents than how it is represented. If the object of representation is sufficiently exalted then the form will follow in grandeur. For all Hegel's talk of coming to self-consciousness, he is not overly smitten with the notion of sharing one's proper journey. We do not know what he thought his particular roles should be with respect to Culture but we can infer important possibilities by examining what he does with respect to three areas of culture: art, religion, and philosophy itself.

Art

The lectures on aesthetics serve as the text book for the first term in the final stage of Hegelian system. That is, Absolute Spirit has as its starting point Art. This is fairly problematic given the lectures themselves. For one thing, Hegel pretty much gives up on the future of art. The really good art was produced during the classical period and while the poetry is still okay, he doesn't sound hopeful for the future.

More seriously, it is hard to see how he could hold otherwise. Culture has been sublated into higher forms of consciousness and the definitions of art that he finds convincing accord with art that is for its own sake and can't be used for moral or other purpose. Additionally he is sensitive to the fact that art mirrors the best of its age and that it cannot help but do this. (The artist cannot decide to operate outside the bounds of historical necessity.) All that is left is revealed religion and philosophy. Like many aestheticians, he is not gaga over art that aspires to being philosophical. Revealed religion does not have a lot of matter to represent. Let's look at what he says in his own words.

> Fine art is not real art till it is in this sense free, and only achieves its highest task when it has taken its place in the same sphere with religion and philosophy, and has become simply a mode of revealing to consciousness and bringing to utterance the Divine Nature, the deepest interests of humanity,

and the most comprehensive truths of the mind. It is in works of art that nations have deposited the profoundest intuitions and ideas of their hearts; and fine art is frequently the key— with many nations there is no other—to the understanding of their wisdom and their religion (*Introductory Lectures on the Aesthetics*, p. 9).

So far so good. Hegel gives us the description of what art is that we should expect from the system. But a few pages later he does not sound melancholy when he announces: "art is, and remains for us, on the side of its highest destiny, a thing of the past" (*Introductory Lectures on the Aesthetics*, p. 13). It looks as if art is over and there is nothing we can do about it because art ceases to be art if it called upon to do any duty, such as be in the service of morality. So we can appreciate past art and see it as holding the place in culture that it does. One of the most careful commentators on Hegel's aesthetics, Michael Inwood, gives the most charitable read when he has Hegel vacillating between two positions: "Hegel wavers between these two positions: that history has exhausted all its possibilities [for art], and that it has exhausted all the possibilities presently conceivable" (p.xxxii).

Returning to the roles that a philosopher plays in the analysis of culture, we might do well to take Hegel very seriously indeed. What if the last works of art were created a very long time ago? What does it say about our culture and the modes of production that parade as knowing more about what art is and is not than those who refuse to consume it? How might it help us account for endlessly recycled theater and film? These are questions posed from within Hegel's perspective. We could add a question he could not have asked how post-Enlightenment are we? In any case Hegel follows the role he has tacitly taken for himself. He describes what is the case about art according to the categories of his system.

Revealed Religion

While Hegel does not hold out much hope for the future of art, he does for revealed religion so we will pay more close attention to what he says both about it and about his relation to it. As Westphal notes,

For while Hegel is by no means the first to whom the ever-problematic concept 'Christian philosopher' can be applied, however problematically, he is the first to lay claim to the even more troublesome title of 'Protestant philosopher' (Westphal, p. 149).

Hegel is specifically and vociferously Lutheran. We saw in the political theory that he is not interested in mixing religion and politics whether that religion is Christian or not: "For Hegel the concept of a Christian or Jewish or Islamic state is a contradiction in terms" (Westphal, p. 161). Revealed religion is Protestant and it is philosophical. The philosopher's role seems to be twofold. To express in philosophical terms what revealed religion is, and to maintain the purviews of its concrete manifestations philosophically. Westphal opines,

> In our own day we have reason to be disturbed by the rise of popular movements that combine a theocratic approach to a variety of moral issues under the general heading of the family with the loud blessings of civil religion on the essentially secular military and economic postures of a nation which wants to maintain a monopoly of power and wealth. We have just as much reason, I believe, to be dismayed by the secularized society to which these movements are a response. This society not only identifies the good with power, pleasure, and wealth, but in doing so adopts a wholly instrumentalized concept of reason, reducing morality to the single maxim that the end justifies the means.
>
> Hegel's ambitious interpretation of the Reformation puts before us the relatively easy task of saying no to these alternatives and the extraordinarily difficult task of finding an alternative (Westphal, p. 163).

Westphal's analysis seems right to me. One's fears about the popular movements he alludes to are properly understood politically, but the culture which gives rise to them must also be addressed for any kind of productive understanding. Let's examine the nature of revealed religion for Hegel and then return to the philosopher's role in the analysis of the culture that espouses secular and religious movements in the manner described by Westphal.

Hegel is very careful to present the revealed religion without reference to any event that would or even could be contrary to History. In the following passage he begins the revealed religion with the belief having entered history that God existed in this world:

> Consciousness, then, does not start from *its* inner life, from thought, and unite *within itself* the thought of God with

66

existence; on the contrary, it starts from an existence that is immediately present and recognizes God therein (*Phenomenology,* 758, p. 458).

What is found when this belief becomes closer and then identical with scientific thought is that what is divine is in each spirit. God is present, immediately, in individuals. The belief that God was one man is supplanted with that that God is in each individual. People wanted this to be the case:

> Here, therefore, God is revealed as He is;...He is immediately present as Spirit...It is precisely this that the revealed religion knows. The hopes and expectations of the world up till now had pressed forward solely to this revelation to behold what absolute Being is, and in it to find itself (*Phenomenology,* 761, p. 461).

Spirit must enter the world absolutely and picture thinking avails us of the story of creation. Nature is revealed to be infused with spirit just as individuals are revealed as possessing Spirit.

> Thus the merely eternal or abstract Spirit becomes an 'other' to itself, or enters into existence, and directly into immediate existence. Accordingly, it creates a world (*Phenomenology,* 774, p. 467).

Once we think creation, either in its primary picture thinking manner or in the manner of revealed religion, we must deal with the problem of evil. Revealed religion is in accord with speculative philosophy that each thing contains its opposites. Evil is no less present in Spirit than Good. Evil is in individuals as it is in Spirit.

> Good and Evil were the specific differences yielded by the thought of Spirit as immediately existent. Since their antithesis has not yet been resolved and they are conceived of as the essence of thought, each of them having an independent existence of its own, man is a self lacking any essential being and is the synthetic ground of their existence and their conflict (*Phenomenology,* 777, p. 469).

Revealed religion requires a community. The representation of the death and resurrection of the God Man is a reminder of the reasons for being a community and for the divinity in the world.

> The death of the divine Man, as death, is abstract negativity, the immediate result of the movement which ends only in natural universality. Death loses this natural meaning in spiritual self-consciousness, i.e. it comes to be its just stated Notion; death becomes transfigured from its immediate meaning, viz. the non-being of this particular individual, into the universality of the Spirit who dwells in His community, dies in it every day, and is daily resurrected (*Phenomenology*, 784, p. 475).

Revealed religion makes no promises about the future but offers a place for both community and love.

> The world is indeed implicitly reconciled with the divine Being; and regarding the divine Being it is known, of course, that it recognizes the object as no longer alienated from it but as identical with it in its love (*Phenomenology*, 787, p. 478).

Hegel describes what he sees as the development of religious thinking to this point and sees the crucial features as being the coming together of the divine and the human, although not at any particular time in history, the subsumption of Evil into Absolute, and the importance of religious community as a place to remember that death is not the final negation—although the promises tied thereto are for Hegel left unspoken. Indeed much else is left unspoken. Hegel sees the role of the philosopher here to be the expositing in the most rational terms what believers in Revealed Religion already know.

To return to Merold Westphal's plea that we examine the prevailing beliefs of our own times and the development of the more powerful ones to their roots including reactions to cultural malaise, I will only add that it seems far preferable to have philosophers detail the history of religious and other cultural thoughts, holding them to methodological scrutiny, and no matter what they to find to continue their thousand year tradition of (mostly) championing the separation of church and state.

Philosophy

In a delightfully titled book *Hegel After Derrida,* Stuart Barnett writes "Hegel revealed that it is the task of philosophy to write the history of the empirical" (Barnett, p. 9). And in our travels with Hegel so far it seems that Hegel has done just that. Revealed religion and art are both taken up into the final phase of Hegel's system: Philosophy. The text he would have us read there is *Lectures on the History of Philosophy.* The philosopher has as one of the roles in analyzing culture knowing the route ideas take to find the form in which they are given to her or him. This seems like a role immanently worthy of keeping. With much of the exciting work being done in Cultural Studies and Post-Structuralism, there is a Hegelian legacy of paying close attention to not so much the historicity of texts but the texts themselves and the traces of themselves back to the ancients.

While this short book cannot offer the sort of attention any thinker deserves prior to mounting criticism, we have examined enough that the criticisms will be fair. And while there is much to admire in Hegel and a universe to learn from him, there is much that must be overcome.

5

Hegel's Critics

Hegel's critics are varied and many. They include Luce Irigary, Friedrich Nietzsche, Soren Kierkegaard, Karl Marx, and Julia Kristeva. And that is not mentioning Jacques Derrida, Michel Foucault, Giles Deleuze, Iris Young, and so many others. For reasons of space I will be dealing with those critics who engage in dialectics with Hegel. There are philosophers who either revere him past what is reasonable and others who just reject him out of hand. His method precludes blind allegiance unless one views his system as so perfect that one is willing to spend the rest of one's scholarly life elaborating the system and filling in the details.

His apologists are found in high government ranks in more than one state. A non-philosophical study of Hegel would have to take those works and the results of them into account. Hegel's influence on international law, historical interpretations of world conflict, and actual policy making with respect to issues as diverse as state welfare and business management, is too large for this study. Furthermore, Hegel's position with respect to the role of the philosopher in the analysis of culture would require that we take each position and study it thoroughly and historically.

Those who reject him out of hand are similarly diverse. One can decide, finally, that Hegel is not one's cup of tea, but facile rejections overlook the need to engage with him if one is to understand the culture in which one finds oneself. With Hegel one finds oneself at moments wanting to reject him. One can get caught up in the majesty of the system, and then, as we noted in chapter two realize that, for example, he has summarily excluded women from civil society. It is not as easy to continue to read Hegel in the ways that we can continue to read other philosophers who similarly exclude women. In his case, he should have known better. One of the reasons I included the time line in chapter one is to indicate that concrete reality over which Hegel claims to have an absolute and scientific view, was not a time when women were silent about their exclusions. Why was this activity invisible to him? Significantly too, why is he so clear to maintain the inclusions he does structurally?

Perhaps even more important than what Hegel should or should not have known, is that Hegel is making absolute claims. One can do a great deal of fancy logical footwork and save the system for women—women can attain absolute spirit individually, just not collectively, the system can be doctored toward inclusion, etc. Still, one wonders, what if Hegel had actually noticed women as subjects?

Another kind of criticism that makes one want to throw up one's hands and find philosophical guidance elsewhere is the relentless movement of system. French philosopher Giles Deleuze does just that. Uninterested in a system that allows one path to freedom, he creates elaborate anti-systems which refuse at every term the category of negation.

One of the most difficult problems with which to deal is the placement of Protestant, Germanic, Christianity at the endpoint of History. We have seen that Kojeve, for instance, sees this move as spelling the end of traditional theism: the age of humanity has been ushered in. There are other manners of reading the text all of which are too complicated to go into detail here. There is much written on the exclusion of whole cultures from the possibility of historical self-consciousness within the system.

I refer readers to an essay I find to be a very good starting point. Robert Bernasconi in "Hegel at the Court of the Ashanti" deals with one specific case in the Hegelian corpus, some of the criticism around it, and importantly the reasons philosophers have found it so hard to acknowledge these problems head on. Bernasconi does in this article what must be done with respect to Hegel's treatment of cultures he antecedently judged lacking: (1) examine the actual things Hegel wrote; (2) examine what was available to Hegel at the time of his writing and what he had both knew and should have known about the cultures he dismissed, and (3) hold contemporary scholars accountable for apologizing for Hegel on these points.

I recommend it as a starting point for examining this problem and as an example of criticism that takes its job seriously.

A reader may be thinking at this point, that in the introductory section "Why Study Hegel?" some mention might have been made of the exclusionary tendency in the system. Why wait until now? The reader may legitimately ask. The three reasons given in the section, that he articulates a existential thesis about the meaning of life worth our study, that his conversation with Kant dominates much twentieth century philosophy, and that Hegel changes the role of the philosopher with respect to culture in crucial ways, hold. He is the sort of thinker that we cannot overlook even if we so choose. As Derrida says "We will never be finished with the reading or the rereading of Hegel, and, in a certain way, I do nothing other than explain myself on this point."

I do not want to suggest that what we should do is any form of "sexism aside" or "racism aside," or "totalitarianism aside." Instead, we must note what in our thinking mirrors what is bad, and take up only those portions that are good, insofar as we are capable of making those judgments. Because of the complications with critical readings that are either too devoted to Hegel and which reject him over hastily, we will confine ourselves to criticisms that are strictly philosophical. That is to say we will look at criticism that tries to modify the system without losing all of it.

I will look at four criticisms that share a central thread: that Hegel's description of reality leave out something so crucial that the dialectical will not be able to proceed without major modification.

Kierkegaard is amazed that Hegel thinks he can speak for absolute spirit. What is left out, according to Kierkegaard, is the impenetrability of God and the essentially private communications a person has with God. If those communications are capable of direct communication, they must be false. Thus Kierkegaard is not immune to the powers of dialectical thinking but he will not allow such thinking to be applied to God.

Irigaray points out that Hegel's erasure of sexual difference causes ontological problems from which the system cannot recover without completely re-thinking its starting point. As she does with many philosophical frameworks, she shows what the system would look like minus the exclusion of sexual difference, and, specifically "woman."

I collapse several criticisms into a section called "Communication of Difference." Philosophers have argued that because Hegelian system gives too much power to negation, the principle of identity cannot contain difference as he argues that it does.

Finally, we will look at Marx's revolutionary inversion of Hegelian system. An easy reading of Marx is to say that he makes the system material, in opposition to the ideal ontology Hegel accords it. Also important is the way in which Marx challenges Hegel's view of the role of the philosopher. Marx sees Hegel as a philosopher who thinks philosophers can only explain the world; Marx argues that philosophy changes it.

Systematic Christianity?

Soren Kierkegaard may be Hegel's harshest critic in the category to which we have confined ourselves. His criticism might be dismissed by some philosophers as an *ad hominen* argument. That is, Hegel is said to be a bad Christian and describing a Christian reality that is subsequently not Christian. The work we will look at, familiarly called the postscript, and fully titled *Concluding Unscientific Postscript,* is postscript to an earlier work called *Philosophical Fragments.* One could almost stop with the titles and be done with the analysis. Kierkegaard is both too much fun and too important to just stop there. Hegel is engaged in a scientific endeavor and hardly thinks that philosophy can be done in fragments. A postscript to fragments as a criticism of him is stylistically and fundamentally a challenge to the very basis of his work.

The postscript poses two problems: that of objective Christianity "what is its truth?" and that of subjective Christianity "How may I, Johannes Climacus, participate in the happiness promised by Christianity?" Johannes Climacus is the pseudonym Kierkegaard assigns himself for this book. In addressing both problems Kierkegaard's sharp wit and elegant writing style are pointed at numerous thinkers. No thinker is more maligned than Hegel.

Kierkegaard is anti-system; his book which is far more than five hundred pages long, starts with the objective problem. This portion of the book ends on page fifty-five The solution to the problem what is the truth of objective Christianity is that Christianity is not the sort of thing that allows of objective study since it is a religion of utmost interiority.

Two points here are worth stressing. The first is his criticism that the manner in which Hegel expresses the revealed religion makes it impossible that he could personally commit one way or the other. Christianity is the sort of thing, for Kierkegaard, to which one commits. Hegel's refusal to show his person in his work is a blow against his profession to be the scribe of the true revealed religion. If Hegel were right, furthermore, Kierkegaard believes that one could not profess to be a Christian even if one were not Hegel. The community Hegel describes for this function could not be more unchristian for Kierkegaard. A body of persons discussing the crucifixion and resurrection rationally is not what makes it true nor what gives it existential meaning.

Furthermore, pace Kierkegaard, Hegel views Christianity as a historical phenomenon and not only arising in history but evolving throughout it. Kierkegaard cannot abide this view. When we looked at revealed religion, it became clear that what is important to Hegel is not whether there is an historical figure who took divinity and humanity into itself. What matters to Hegel is that as that belief becomes more and more rational from simple picture-thinking to faith to pure intuition to the representations through revealed religion. Kierkegaard expresses his reaction against the position by simply asking what if Christianity were not historical.

He is not worried about criticism of this position, admitting that people will probably say of him "How stupid! What an extraordinary hankering after originality to say such a thing, especially now, when philosophy has arrived at an understanding of the necessity of the historical" (Kierkegaard, p. 52). Kierkegaard takes the eternality of Christianity very seriously. In *The Concept of Irony,* he argues that Socrates has the qualities of a Christian—a historical position Hegel could not respect.

So the objective problem is solved and Kierkegaard moves on to the subjective problem. We saw Kojeve acquiescing in Hegel's pronouncement that he had seen absolute knowledge. Kierkegaard is less charitable:

> Being an individual man is a thing that has been abolished, and every speculative philosopher confuses himself with humanity at large; whereby he becomes infinitely great, and at the same time nothing at all. He confounds himself with humanity in sheer distraction of mind, just as the opposition press urges the royal "we," and sailors say: "devil may take me!" But when a man has indulged in oaths for a long time, he returns at last to the simple utterance, because all swearing is self-nugatory; and when one discovers that every street urchin can say "we," one perceives that it means a little more, after all, to be a particular individual. And when one finds that every cellar-dweller can play the game of being humanity, one learns at last, that being purely and simply a human being

is a more significant thing than playing the society game in this fashion. And one thing more. When a cellar-dweller plays this game everyone thinks it ridiculous; and yet it is equally ridiculous for the greatest man in the world to do it. And one may very well permit oneself to laugh at him for this, while still entertaining a just and proper respect for his talents and his learning, and so forth (Kierkegaard, p. 113).

His critique here is that the sort of knowledge that Hegel is claiming is just silly. "Reality itself is a system—for God; but it cannot be a system for any existing spirit" (Kierkegaard, p. 107). He expounds a positive view that there are three spheres of existence for individuals: aesthetic, ethical and religious. These realms are not connected by necessity nor does any individual or historical period have to pass from one to the other either in order or even at all. One could be in the aesthetic realm for the whole of one's life. Instead of the relentless moving of Spirit from one stage to another according to the rules of reason, the movement in Kierkegaard's system occurs from the inside, when an individual decides to take the plunge. We move through Kierkegaard's realms by leaps of faith.

For Hegel, of course the system moves with the concept of negation. Thus, e.g. the Enlightenment moves forward to morality because the heaviness of its contradictions spawns violence which requires moral consciousness to reassert itself. Kierkegaard criticizes the form of this general movement in two ways. First, in confronting every bit of objective knowledge, one encounters this truth: there is only approximation knowledge. Historical knowledge in particular cannot be known with certainty because the richness of its concrete detail escapes specificity. Second, Hegel is aware of the multiplicity of phenomena. This is why he answers Kant as he does with a subject who exists necessarily as objective and objects that match up with subjects through their jointly ideal status. Kierkegaard answers like this:

> The positiveness of historical knowledge is illusory, since it is approximation-knowledge; the speculative result is a delusion. For all this positive knowledge fails to express the situation of the knowing subject in existence. It concerns rather a fictitious objective subject, and to confuse oneself with such a subject is to be duped...Nothing historical can become infinitely certain for me except the fact of my own existence (which again cannot become infinitely certain for any other

individual, who has infinite certainty only of his own existence), and this is not something historical (Kierkegaard, p. 75).

The book ends with Johannes Climacus telling his readers that he will not say that he is a Christian because it certainly appears to him that it is far too difficult to be a Christian. This may be the most pointedly directed criticism of all. Being a Christian for Kierkegaard does mean going to church, being in a religious community, or thinking about the meaning of God: instead it means living a life while in indirect communication with God.

Sexual Difference

Before turning to Irigaray's criticism of Hegel, I quote a passage from the introduction to a book called *Derrida and Feminism*. In this introduction it is made clear that to deal with Derrida, one must first deal with Hegel and to deal with either philosopher one must address the extent of exclusion of women from Hegelian system:

> Hegel makes this decision of the question intrinsic to the self-unfolding of Absolute Spirit: both to its self reflection in language and to its embodiment in practical activity and social forms. To the woman belongs the care of the body and blood, the domain of the family and funeral rites. To the man, whose body the woman properly tends—as Antigone tends first her father, then her brother—belongs the public domains of action, science, politics, and philosophy. Even language, the universalizing medium, is said to be foreign or opaque to her. The system of Absolute System depends upon this division of labor and life (Feder, Rawlinson, Zakin, pp. 1-2).

The points made above are crucial. Hegel does not pay attention to the importance of women coming to know themselves as women occurring all around him during the time he was writing. (If he does he does not find it of systemic importance.) He excludes from the movement to absolute spirit at the point where the family dissolves itself to move into civil society. He suffers a second blind spot when he then fails to realize that even though there is henceforth silence about sexual

76

division, every other institution is dependent on the material reality of the women left behind. This criticism is important because it does not deviate from Hegel's terms nor methodology. What we leave behind stays with us in the next stage in some other form. With that thought in mind let us turn to the analysis of French philosopher and psychoanalyst Luce Irigaray:

> The only possible way of reconciling objective spirit and absolute spirit seems to be to rethink the notion of gender, of the genders, and of their ethical relationships. This will modify the data in presence. Objective spirit will no longer be made up of the head and trunk, the spirit and the body that are bonded together so poorly that growth depends upon periodic wars, suppressions, destructions, and sublations—assuming that any bonding has in fact occurred in History; the record of the latest philosophers rather indicates the contrary. Hegel also insists on the fact that the spirit had never really entered into History, thus concurring with the pessimistic view Freud and others have held about civilization (Irigaray, pp. 141-142).

Irigaray's criticism is sophisticated. Her argument is that much of the strife implicated throughout system is due to the ex-appropriation of female materiality in the silent manner Hegel performs. The data to which she is referring have to do with revealed religion among other things. For instance, the historical figure of Jesus Christ as the data comes to us, did not separate himself from women. This information is missing from Hegelian system because for him the actual fact of Jesus Christ is also missing. (We saw in chapter four that indeed for Hegel spirit does not enter history in fact but through repetitive picture thinking.) The absence of sexual difference in system is not an isolated philosophical datum particular to Hegel.

Because of his exclusion, the exclusion continues throughout, for instance, much of phenomenology. Thus Heidegger in *Being and Time* pays no heed to sexual difference in either ontological or ontic terms. Hegel's erasure has implications that permeate twentieth-century, and indeed twenty-first-century thinking. It is important that this omission was not necessary to his time. Ultimately Plato erases sexual difference but even Plato spent considerable energy thinking about sexual difference.

· For an encyclopedic thinker such as Hegel this failure to pay attention to the evidence not only of his senses but of the historical reality which precedes him and surrounds him, necessitates a kind of

77

violent rupture from his own method and the reality he describes. The overly violent nature of his system may be inevitable based on his refusal to consider sexual difference as a fundamental category of analysis and observation.

Irigaray's criticism is crucial for thinkers today. It is often portrayed in culture that "what women want" is equality. Hegel's system shows us that equality is as problematic as any other universal. What women could be said to want is merely to exist within the cultural structures that form the consciousness of the world. In an essay on Spinoza Irigaray asks us to consider what if "woman" existed. (Notice that the consideration is not what if individual women existed, which of course they do. Instead the consideration asked of us is what if women were theorized as other than the material from which men think.)

Her criticism is radical in the truest sense of the word. What if we stopped pretending that we could solve problems of violence against the other by further pretending that the word "man" for existence means men and women?

Communication of Difference

One of the Hegel's primary hypotheses regarding the structure of human experience is that the development of individual consciousness recapitulates the development of historical consciousness, or, as it was commonly expressed in the nineteenth century, ontogenesis mirrors phylogenesis. Of course, this hypothesis, as well as its particular interpretations, hardly stands beyond empirical critique. My strategy is to read the phenomenology of self-consciousness not as an abstract deduction of concepts nor as contingent chronology but as a psychohistory, and in particular as a psychohistory that accounts for both ontogenetic and phylogenetics events that might explain dominant expressions of the masculinized self in Western Culture...While these allegiances reflect dominant and recurrent themes in Western Eurocentric culture, they are not universal. On the contrary, I shall argue that Hegel's uncritical appropriation of these themes reinforces asymmetries of power that his dialectic otherwise aims to overcome (Willett, p. 107).

Cynthia Willett begins her discussion of Hegel with the criticism that Hegel is struggling with the task of ending gross abuses of power.

Because he uncritically takes up the categories of European discourse (some commentators would narrow his taking up to the categories of Germanic discourse) he is unable to achieve absolute knowledge. Instead what he is able to achieve is the erection of a monument to the psychological state of European man in the nineteenth century. That in itself is interesting. It becomes dangerous when it purports to describe the entire world.

Subjects who do not speak and think like the model presented through Hegel, pace Willett, cannot be heard through the clatter of falsely ascribed universals. Thus the Christian who follows Kierkegaard's anti-systemic route to Christianity is disenfranchised. The woman who chooses a role in civil society does so at the risk of losing what is special to her about being woman as opposed to man. Willett argues that a careful reading of Hegel shows that he cannot account for the voice toward freedom of Fredrick Douglass.

In his narrative of his coming to freedom, a narrative which should according to the structure of Hegelian system, stand as a pinnacle of spirit coming to know itself as spirit complete with the conflict to own language and culture, there are elements which cannot be accounted for by system. I will mention here only Douglass's attention to the loving care he received from his grandmother as an impetus toward and power to find freedom. So the exclusions disallow the very sort of account it purports to explain.

Other voices which are unable to speak with Hegelian system include those who are willing to accept the dialectic but not the final end point of history as either that Hegel pinpoints or a final end at all. This latter group are those who hear terror when they hear slogans such as "Finish the Revolution" or "Freedom Fighters for Democracy" both of which have roots in Hegelian thought. Some noted thinkers here include George Bataille and Friedrich Nietzsche.

For Bataille the major problem with Hegel is that his category of negation is so strong that there is nothing left over. That is, he thinks that Hegel has created an economy without reserve. Everything has already exhausted itself, there is no extra for those things we celebrate and consign to the sacred. Bataille struggles with a method to counter negation and comes up with a philosophical category he picks up from Kierkegaard (with whom he says he identifies with to the point of self-identification!)--laughter. At the point where negation threatens to nullify those things in life which make us uniquely who we are, that is in our most radical interiority, Bataille says he can only explode with laughter.

Nietzsche is more Hegelian than he sometimes allows. There is much written on his interesting relationship to Hegel. A point of radical departure involves the role of history. Nietzsche writes an essay entitled "On the Advantages and Disadvantages of History for Life," in which he delineates several kinds of history. He calls for a critical history and urges that in the education of the young, history be taught in a different manner than the Hegelian manner. He worries that a nihilism will result from an unaltered Hegelian history that will most likely turn cynical. He prefers that when faced with the run of inevitable history, the response would be a sort of irony he finds missing in Hegel. It is interesting that Kierkegaard too finds Hegel utterly lacking in irony.

While many have found Hegel unable to accommodate the many and diverse voices which make up our global set of nation-states and corporations, others find him useful, not only for a model of deliberative rational communication that might settle difference he did not see, but also for urging for states which value rationality over public opinion, fear, raw power, and religion. Fred Dallmayr argues:

> One of the important legacies of Hegel's philosophy is the stress on the institutionalization of *sittlichkeit* (Ethical Life) and especially on the embodiment or 'incorporation' of public spirit in a 'universal class'—a stress later adapted by Marx on economic premises. Honoring the intent (though not the letter of this legacy), I see the need for a renewed and more radical adaptation. Under democratic auspices, I believe, embodiment of public spirit can no longer be located in either a bureaucracy or a class, but only in plural and heterogeneous groupings cross-cutting social divisions (or inhabiting the margins of such divisions) (Dallmayr, p. 341).

Dallmayr's pragmatic approach, taking the good from a flawed system, is Hegelian in spirit and is timely.

Revolutionary Inversions

Karl Marx is often said to have taken up Hegel in method but turned what was ideal material thereby creating the unexpected child of Hegel and Marx: dialectical materialism or historical materialism. Briefly put, historical materialism is the theory that history is the history of class struggle. In any given society there are two major classes, those who produce things and those who own them. During the time period during which Marx was writing the producing class was the proletarian class and the owning class was the capitalist class. Whatever the historical period the owning class is the ruling class and the producing class is the working class. Inevitably these two classes will fight, to the death if necessary, over the means of production. The owning class believes itself to have the right of ownership and will do everything in its power to maintain the most power over the means of production. The producing class becomes increasingly conscious of itself as the producer of value and will thereby do everything in its power to get more control over the means of production.

Throughout history the producing class becomes increasingly conscious of itself in that role. Eventually the producing class will overthrow the owning class completely and there will be the end of history because we cannot imagine what it would be like to be in a world without this central struggle. There will only be one class and this class will produce together and in social concert true science, sometimes referred to as proletarian science. This will be a true science because it will be science which has as its aim the improvement of all humanity and not that of filling the coffers of capitalists.

The Hegelian element in what was briefly described is obvious. Still, the reader must be thinking that Hegel would not be thrilled with this use of his work. In the criticism I will delineate from Marx one can see that Marx is a respectful critic, although not always a polite one. In describing historical materialism the astute reader will have noticed that no mention was made of the state. This is because for Marx, when the final class battle is fought, the state will wither away. He is far less concerned with the state (the locus of politics) than he is with society. Concerning ourselves with government is not cost-effective. They do not control much of anything according to Marx but work at the behest of the ruling class. This is enough background to address the two criticisms of Marx at hand.

The first involves the manner in which philosophers might talk with one another and with the public. Marx, unlike Hegel, was a brilliant rhetorician. When he was writing for members of the unions, or addressing them, he used a different kind of language than he did when he was writing *Das Kapital*. The tones he takes in his letters is also appropriate for what he wants and from whom. These elements are understood when writing this criticism.

Vulgar criticism falls into an opposite dogmatic error. Thus, for example, it criticizes the constitution, drawing attention to the opposition of the powers, etc. It finds contradictions everywhere. But criticism that struggles with its opposite remains dogmatic criticism, as for example in earlier times, when the dogma of the Blessed Trinity was set aside by appealing to the contradiction between 1 and 3. True criticism, however, shows the internal genesis of the Blessed Trinity in the human brain. It describes the act of its birth. Thus, true philosophical criticism of the present state constitution not only shows the contradictions as existing, but explains, them, grasps their essence and necessity. It comprehends their own proper significance. However, this comprehension does not, as Hegel thinks, consist in everywhere recognizing the determinations of the logical concept, but rather grasping the proper logic of the proper object (Marx, p. 92).

This is a clever piece of writing manifesting Marx's usual wit and humor. The main point of this passage is that Hegel makes a very bad mistake in thinking that he can understand the world by imposing logic on everything in it. Instead he should focus on determining what is the case logically about objects of inquiry. There are two substantial criticisms embedded in the criticism of method.

The first is that while Hegel is not dogmatic in his criticisms of the constitution, he misses what is important about its genesis and execution because he does not look at how it really arises in life. This is complicated and Marx knows it. He has argued that Hegel misses the material reality which gives birth to any given constitution and that the constitution will never be the real truth about a state unless the state represents each person in similar fashion. (The truth of any state is democracy, argues Marx, and we haven't seen that yet because you can't write it or think it, you have to have it.)

The second criticism is structurally similar. Hegel gets all caught up in Spirit because noticing only the logical structure of what the very educated have said about it, he refuses to acknowledge that the story told about spirit is that Mary gave birth to Jesus. Hegel cannot talk about this philosophically.

The religious, political and social criticisms come combined like this because Marx sees all of these modes of consciousness as arising from real conflict. His criticism shows that Hegel's "mistakes" are due to his positing the conflicts as flowing from the theories.

82

The second criticism I will address from Marx concerns Hegel's getting something right for the wrong reasons. It is a lengthy passage but worth seeing in its entirety:

> Hegel calls private rights the rights of abstract personality, or abstract rights. And indeed they have to be developed as the abstraction, and thus the illusory rights, of abstract personality, just as the moral doctrine developed by Hegel is the illusory existence of abstract subjectivity. Hegel develops private rights and morals as abstractions, from which it does not follow, for him, that the state or ethical life of which they are the presuppositions can be nothing but the society (the social life) of these illusions; rather, he concludes that they are subalternate moments of this ethical life. But what are private rights except the rights of these subjects of the state, and what is morality except their morality? In other words, the person of private rights and the subject of morals are the person and the subject of the state. Hegel has been widely criticized for his development of morality. He has done nothing but develop the morality of the modern state and modern private rights. A more complete separation of morality from the state, its fuller emancipation, was desired. What did that prove except that the separation of the present-day state from morals is moral, that morals are non-political and that the state is not moral? It is rather a great, though from one aspect (namely, from the aspect that Hegel declares the state, whose presupposition is such a morality, to be the realistic idea of ethical life) an unconscious service of Hegel to have assigned to modern morality its true position (Marx, pp. 108-109).

This is a devastating criticism. Marx argues that by putting private rights and morals into abstraction, and then allowing the state a full super-session of them, Hegel instead of insuring morality for it, gives it license to be other than moral. It is a stronger case than this, however. Not only does the state lose its socio-political justification and hence obligation to act morally, it is told that so losing it is in fact moral.

When we compared Marx and Kant on political theory we noted that Kant holds the state to the categorical imperative by having a constitution which is consistent with its formulations. By contrast Hegel does not bind his state to morality and indeed sees no need to do so. Marx reveals that in this case, Hegel is true to his method of describing what is the case. For Marx, the state is an arm of ruling class interests and as such knows no morals except that of carrying out the private rights of the ruling class. The state will do everything in its power to enforce those rights including classifying private rights so that they will never include labor itself as a property right. Thus private rights are enforced but without the gentle nudging of morality whose place has been relegated, as has religion's to the "merely" social realm. Marx has the irony that Nietzsche claims Hegel does not have. He is not seriously misrepresenting Hegel but we can be quite sure that yet again Hegel is not going to be delighted with this interpretation.

Marx pays allegiance to Hegel by not including morality in his analysis of the state nor in his analysis of the relations between ruling and producing classes. Indeed, he argues that morality itself is class dependent with bourgeois morality differing substantially from proletarian.

Conclusion

The criticisms in this chapter only scratch the surface of what has been written for and against Hegel. It remains the case in 2000 that many of us feel obliged when rethinking a position to check it against Hegel. I think that the selection is sufficiently varied that the reader have a good idea of the sorts of discussions Hegel has occasioned and continues to occasion.

Bibliography

Barnett, Stuart, editor. *Hegel After Derrida*. New York: Routledge, 1998.

Beiser, Frederick C. *The Cambridge Companion to Hegel*. Cambridge: Cambridge University Press, 1993.

Bernasconi, Robert. "Hegel at the Court of the Ashanti," in *Hegel After Derrida*, pp. 41-63.

Booth, William James. *Interpreting the World, Kant's Philosophy of History and Politics*. Toronto: University of Toronto Press, 1986.

Cutrofello, Andrew. *The Owl at Dawn: A Sequel to Hegel's Phenomenology of Spirit*. Albany: State University of New York Press.

Dallmayr, Fred. "Rethinking the Hegelian State," in *Hegel and Legal Theory*, Drucilla Cornell, Michel Rosenfeld and David Gray Carlson, editors. New York: Routledge, 1991.

Feder, Ellen K., Mary C. Rawlinson, nad Emily Zakin , Introduction to *Derrida and Feminism*. New York: Routledge, 1997.

Harris, H.S. *Hegel: Phenomenology and System*. Indianapolis: Hackett, 1995.

Hegel, G.F.W. *Introductory Lectures on Aesthetics*. Translated by Bernard Bosanquet. London: Penguin Books, 1993.

----------. *Lectures on the History of Philosophy: Plato and the Platonists*, Volume 2. Translated by E.S. Haldane and Frances H. Simson. Lincoln: University of Nebraska Press, 1995.

----------. *Logic*. Translated by William Wallace. Oxford, Clarendon Press, 1975.

----------. *Philosophy of History*. Translated by J. Sibree.

New York: Dover Publications, Inc, 1956.

----------. *Philosophy of Mind.* Translated by A.V. Miller. Oxford: Clarendon Press, 1971.

----------. *Philosophy of Right.* Translated by T.M. Knox. Oxford: Oxford University Press, 1952

----------. *Phenomenology of Spirit.* Translated by A.V. Miller. Oxford: Clarendon Press, 1977.

----------. *Reason in History.* Translated by Robert S. Hartman. Indianapolis: Bobbs-Merrill Company, Inc, 1953.

Hyppolite, Jean. *Genesis and Structure of Hegel's Phenomenology of Spirit.* Translated by Samuel Cherniak and John Heckman. Evanston: Northwestern University Press, 1974.

Inwood, Michael. *A Hegel Dictionary.* Oxford: Blackwell Publishers Ltd, 1992.

Irigaray, Luce. "The Universal as Mediation," in *Sexes and Genealogies.* Translated by Gillian C. Gill. New York: Columbia University Press, 1993.

Jacobson, Arthur J. "Abstract Right and Private Law," in *Hegel and Legal Theory,* Drucilla Cornell, Michel Rosenfeld and David Gray Carlson, editors. New York: Routledge, 1991.

Kainz, Howard P. *G.W.F. Hegel: The Philosophical System.* Athens: Ohio University Press, 1996.

Kant, Immanuel. *Critique of Pure Reason.* Translated by Norman Kemp Smith. New York: St. Martin's Press, 1929.

----------. *Grounding for the Metaphysics of Morals.* Translated by James. W. Ellington. Indianapolis: Hackett, 1981.

----------. *Metaphysical Elements of Justice.* Translated by John Ladd. New York: Macmillan Publishing Company, 1985.

----------. *Perpetual Peace.* Edited by Lewis White Beck. Indianapolis: Bobbs-Merrill, 1957.

Kaufmann, Walter, translator and editor. *Hegel: Texts and Commentary.* Garden City, New York: Anchor Books, 1966.

Kierkegaard, Soren. *Concluding Unscientific Postscript.* Translated by Swenson and Lowrie. Princeton: Princeton University Press, 1947.

Kojeve, Alexandre. *Introduction to the Reading of Hegel.* Assembled by Raymond Queneau, edited by Allan Bloom, translated by James H. Nichols, Jr. Ithaca: Cornell University Press, 1969.

Kolb, David. *The Critique of Pure Modernity: Hegel, Heidegger, and After.* Chicago: The University of Chicago Press, 1986.

Krell, David Farrell. *Son of Spirit: A Novel.* Albany: State University of New York Press, 1997.

Lowenberg, Jacob. *Hegel: Selections.* New York: Scribner's Sons, 1929.

Marx, Karl. *Critique of Hegel's 'Philosophy of Right'.* Translated by Annette Jolin and Joseph O'Malley. Cambridge: Cambridge University Press, 1970.

Shell, Susan Meld. *The Rights of Reason: A Study of Kant's Philosophy and Politics.* Toronto: University of Toronto Press, 1980.

Singer, Peter. *Hegel.* Oxford: Oxford University Press, 1983.

Stepelevich, Lawrence S., editor. *The Young Hegelians.* Cambridge: Cambridge University Press, 1983.

Taylor, Charles. *Sources of the Self.* Cambridge: Harvard University Press, 1989.

----------. *Hegel.* Cambridge: Cambridge University Press, 1975.

Westphal, Merold. *Hegel, Freedom, and Modernity.* Albany: State University of New York Press, 1992.

Willett, Cynthia. *Maternal Ethics and Other Slave Moralities.* New York: Routledge, 1995.

Wolff, Robert Paul. *Kant's Theory of Mental Activity.* Gloucester, Mass.: Peter Smith, 1973.

Zizek, Slavoj. *Tarrying with the Negative: Kant, Hegel, and the Critique of Ideology.* Durham: Duke University Press, 1993).